DARTMOOR'S
Greatest Walk

*A Guide to the Perambulation
of the
Forest of Dartmoor*

Bill Ransom

DEVON BOOKS

First published in Great Britain in 1987 by Devon Books

Copyright © Bill Ransom, 1987

Photographs © Bill Ransom, 1987

ISBN: 0 86114-800-2

British Library Cataloguing-in-Publication Data

Ransom, Bill
    Dartmoor's greatest walk: a guide to the perambulation
of the Forest of Dartmoor
    1. Dartmoor (England)—Description and travel—Guide-books
    I. Title
    914.23′5304858   DA670.D2

Printed and bound in Great Britain by A. Wheaton & Co. Ltd.

DEVON BOOKS

Official Publisher to Devon County Council
Devon Books is a division of A. Wheaton & Co. Ltd, which represents:

Editorial, Design, Publicity, Production and Manufacturing
A. Wheaton & Co. Ltd
Hennock Road, Marsh Barton, Exeter, Devon EX2 8RP
Tel: 0392 74121; Telex 42749 (WHEATN G)
(A. Wheaton & Co. Ltd is a member of the
Pergamon/B.P.C.C. Group of Companies)

Sales and Distribution
Town & Country Books, P.O. Box 31, Newton Abbot, Devon TQ12 5AQ
Tel: 080 47 2690

CONTENTS

ACKNOWLEDGEMENTS

The author is especially grateful to the Duchy of Cornwall for defining the historical boundary of the Forest of Dartmoor, as perceived by them, and helping to resolve points of difficulty.

Thanks are also due to the author's wife for checking the text and sketch-maps for clarity and relevance.

The maps have been drawn from the author's sketch-maps by Ian Foulis and Associates.

The cover photograph shows walkers at Huntingdon Cross on the Forest boundary.

INTRODUCTION

In 1848 Samuel Rowe, Vicar of Crediton, published his *Perambulation of Dartmoor*. This was a description of the antiquities and topography of the Forest of Dartmoor and was dedicated to the Prince of Wales. It must rank as the first work on Dartmoor which could serve as a guide to walkers desirous of exploring the moor. It gave an account of fifteen excursions and a great deal of supporting material. The perambulation of the Forest boundary was encompassed, in broad terms, within the fifteen excursions. It preceded Crossing's famous guide by some sixty years. Rightly considered a classic, Rowe's *Perambulation* has been reissued more than once, the most recent edition being that published by Devon Books in 1985.

Many walking groups and individuals are interested in walking the Forest boundary, following the course believed to have been taken in 1240. Rowe's *Perambulation* was never intended to provide the detail which such walkers would find of most value. Somewhat surprisingly, in view of the extensive literature devoted to Dartmoor, no guide which does so has subsequently been published. The aim of this account is to fill that gap and to draw attention to related features of historical and topographical interest. In so doing, it describes both the boundary accepted by the Duchy of Cornwall as the true historical one and that more generally accepted as the modern boundary. The walker can make his or her choice: the author takes no sides.

The author has walked many times all the stages of the perambulation and every care has been taken to avoid errors and inaccuracies. No responsibility can be taken, however, for any which still exist.

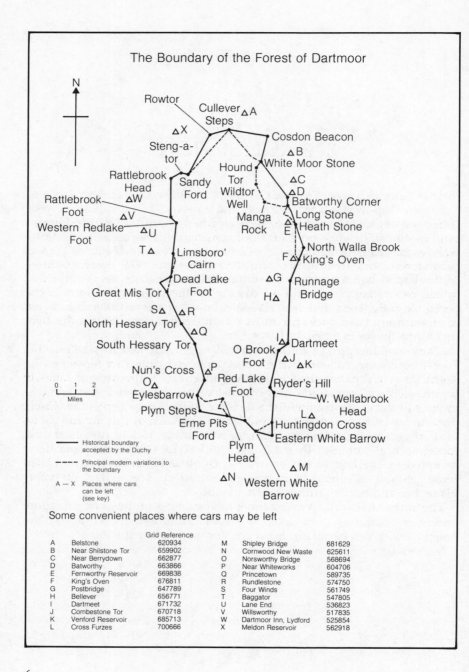

The Boundary of the Forest of Dartmoor

N

Rowtor
Cullever △A
Steps
Cosdon Beacon
△X
Steng-a-tor
△B
White Moor Stone
Hound Tor
Rattlebrook Head
△W
Sandy Ford
Wildtor Well
△C
△D
Batworthy Corner
Rattlebrook Foot
△V
Manga Rock
Long Stone
Heath Stone
△E
Western Redlake Foot
△U
North Walla Brook
T△
Limsboro' Cairn
F△ King's Oven
Dead Lake Foot
△G
Runnage Bridge
Great Mis Tor
H△
S△ △R
North Hessary Tor
△Q
South Hessary Tor
I△
Dartmeet
O Brook Foot
△J △K
Nun's Cross
O△
△P
Red Lake Foot
Ryder's Hill
Eylesbarrow
Z
W. Wellabrook Head
Plym Steps
Erme Pits Ford
L△
Huntingdon Cross
Plym Head
Eastern White Barrow
△M
△N
Western White Barrow

0 1 2
Miles

——— Historical boundary accepted by the Duchy

- - - - Principal modern variations to the boundary

A — X Places where cars can be left (see key)

Some convenient places where cars may be left

		Grid Reference			
A	Belstone	620934	M	Shipley Bridge	681629
B	Near Shilstone Tor	659902	N	Cornwood New Waste	625611
C	Near Berrydown	662877	O	Norsworthy Bridge	568694
D	Batworthy	663866	P	Near Whiteworks	604706
E	Fernworthy Reservoir	669838	Q	Princetown	589735
F	King's Oven	676811	R	Rundlestone	574750
G	Postbridge	647789	S	Four Winds	561749
H	Bellever	656771	T	Baggator	547805
I	Dartmeet	671732	U	Lane End	536823
J	Combestone Tor	670718	V	Willsworthy	517835
K	Venford Reservoir	685713	W	Dartmoor Inn, Lydford	525854
L	Cross Furzes	700666	X	Meldon Reservoir	562918

THE
HISTORICAL CONTEXT

A forest, at least from the time of the Norman Conquest, was designated as Crown land and reserved for the purposes of the chase. As such, it was inhabited and cultivated only by permission of the king. It is a common misconception that a forest must be wooded, though it often was in medieval times. A forest comprised 'vert', i.e. trees, turf and other green vegetation, and 'venison', which was not merely deer but included hare, boar and wolf, designated as beasts of the forest, buck, doe, fox and marten, taken to be beasts of the hunt or chase, and rabbit, pheasant, partridge, quail, mallard and heron, considered to be beasts of the warren.

A forest, however, provided much more than an outlet for royalty to hunt. In particular, much profit was obtained by the levy of taxes in return for permission to pasture cattle and pigs within the forest and to extract wood, bark, peat and stone. Revenue was also derived by fining those who offended against the many clauses comprising the forest law and by granting rights within the forest for a fee. The forest laws were upheld by courts and their judges and officers. Attendance at these courts was onerous and was much resented. Under the early forest laws, particularly those of Henry I, the penalties for killing or stealing game were, by modern standards, barbarous; they included blinding, mutilation and death. A trespasser who resisted the hue and cry could be lawfully killed.

The forests reached their greatest extent in the reign of King John. It is in his reign that the Forest of Dartmoor is first mentioned specifically though the earliest known reference to Dartmoor (Dertemora) appears in a Pipe Roll of 1181. In the sixth year of the reign of King John, on 18th May 1204, a Charter was granted to disafforest all Devonshire 'up to the metes and bounds of Dartmoor and Exmoor'. This Charter, inter alia, provided that all land afforested in the reign of King John should be disafforested. The reasons for the granting of the Charter almost certainly included pressure from the barons and the desire to raise money. This disafforestation of Devon raised five thousand marks for the Crown.

It is not known for certain whether any perambulation of the Forest of Dartmoor was ever made as a result of the granting of that Charter. There is reasonable evidence, however, to suppose that it was for in the next reign, that of Henry III, a writ of 23rd April 1220 commanded the Sheriff of Devon to 'permit Roger de Toeny to hold in peace his land, with its appurtenances, which is in the moor of Dartmoor as it was perambulated in the time of King John our father by his order'. Whether or not perambulations of forests in general were undertaken in or around the year 1204 it seems unlikely that the provisions of that Charter were implemented effectively for in the second year of his reign, on 6th November 1217, Henry III granted another Charter. This disafforested all lands afforested by Richard I and by John except for lands in royal demesne. The Charter was issued in the king's name by William Marshall, Earl of Pembroke, for Henry was then but ten years old. This Charter also greatly softened the severity of the old forest law.

It seems that little of practical significance stemmed from that Charter either. It is probable that the majority of English forests were not perambulated until after the issue of a Statute on 11th February 1224, in the ninth year of the reign of Henry III. This required that 'all Forests which King Henry our grandfather afforested and made shall be viewed by good and lawful men and if he hath made Forest of any wood more than that of his own demesne whereby the owner of the wood hath hurt We will that forthwith it be disafforested saving the common of herbage and of other things in the same Forest to them which before were accustomed to have the same'. It is probable that Dartmoor was then perambulated but there is no record to that effect. (It may be noted that Dartmoor would not have been disafforested by that Statute or by preceding Charters for, being a part of the Borough of Lydford, it was royal demesne. Thus the Domesday entry reads, 'The King has a Borough, Lideford. King Edward held it in demesne.')

By a Charter dated 10th October 1239, Henry III granted to his brother Richard, Earl of Poitou and Cornwall, 'Our Manor of Lydford, with the castle of the same place, and all its appurtenances, together with the Forest of Dartmoor, and all the appurtenances of the same Forest, to hold as freely and quietly as We held it on the day We gave it to him, rendering yearly at the Exchequer £10 for all service, custom and demand'. Once the Forest passed from the king's hands, and failing any successful application for Justices of the Forest to be appointed, it became a Chase. This grant to Richard led to the perambulation of the Forest (strictly the Chase) of Dartmoor. This was carried out in 1240 and provides the earliest record of the boundary between the Forest and the lands of the lords of adjacent manors.

On the death of Edmund, Earl of Cornwall, in 1300 the Forest reverted to the Crown. By a Charter granted in the eleventh year of the reign of Edward III, on 17th March 1337, the king granted the Castle and Manor of Lydford with appurtenances and the Chase of Dartmoor with appurtenances to Edward the Black Prince, Duke of Cornwall. This was the Charter creating the Duchy of Cornwall: the Chase of Dartmoor – still known in common parlance as the Forest of Dartmoor – has been part of the Duchy to the present day.

THE BOUNDARY

On 13th June 1240, a writ was issued by Henry III directing the Sheriff of Devon to summon a jury of twelve knights to determine by perambulation the boundary of the Forest of Dartmoor. The official return to this writ has never been found. There are, however, several copies in existence which vary slightly, but not significantly, from one another. These copies are described in 'Historical Documents Relating to Dartmoor' by Robert Dymond in the *Transactions of the Devonshire Association* (T.D.A.) for the year 1879 (Vol. 11, pp. 371–82). The copy most frequently referred to is that which appears in the Appendix to Rowe's *Perambulation of Dartmoor*, 1856.

William de la Brewer and eleven other knights undertook the perambulation, starting at 'Hoga of Cossdonne and thence lineally to the small Hoga which is called Little Hunde Torre, and thence lineally to Thurlestone, and thence lineally to Wotesbrokelakesfote, which falls in Tyng, and thence lineally to Heighestone, and thence lineally to Langestone, and thence lineally as far as through the middle turbary of Alberysheved, and so along Wallebrok, and thence lineally as far as Furnum Regis, and thence lineally to Wallebrokshede, and so along Wallebrok until it falls into Dart, and so by Dart to another Dart, and so by the other Dart ascending to Okebrokysfote, and so ascending Okebrok to la Dryework, and so ascending to la Dryfeldford, and so lineally to Battyshull, and so lineally to the head of Wester Wellabroke, and so by Wester Wellabroke till it falls into Aven, and thence lineally to Ester Whyteburghe, and thence lineally to la Rede Lake where it falls into Erme, and thence lineally to Grymsgrove, and thence lineally to Elysburghe, and so lineally to Syward's Cross and thence to Ysfother, and so by another Ysfother and thence by the middle of Mystor to Mewyburghe, and thence to Lullingesfote, and thence to Rakerne-brokysfote, and so to the head of the same water, and thence to la West Solle, and thence lineally to Ernestorre, and thence lineally to the next ford on the east side of the Chapel of St. Michael of Halgestoke, and thence lineally to the aforesaid Hoga of Cossdonne on the east part.'

On 15th August 1608, in the sixth year of the reign of James I, another survey of the boundary was carried out which closely paralleled the survey of 1240 but gave some intermediate points and interpreted certain of the names in a manner which has caused much conflict of opinion. Thus Thurlestone was called Waterdontorr, Wotesbrokelakes-fote became Whoodelake, West Solle became Steinegtorr and Arme Headd, Plimheadd, Dedlakeheadd, and Sandyford were added. Over the years there have been many interpretations of the places believed to correspond to these thirteenth- and seventeenth-century names. The most important of these have been by Spence Bate in 1872 (T.D.A. Vol. 5), by Prowse in 1892 (T.D.A. Vol.24) and by Somers-Cocks in 1983 (see Crispin Gill, *Dartmoor: A New Study*).

The Duchy of Cornwall recognizes the historical boundary of the Forest to have been as follows: Cullever Steps – northern tumulus on Cosdon – tumulus on Little Hound Tor – White Moor Stone – boundary rock near Ruelake Pit – Teign-e-ver Clapper – Batworthy Corner – Longstone on Shovel Down – North Walla Brook – along the North Walla Brook past King's Oven to the Walla Brook – East Dart – Dartmeet – along the West Dart to the O Brook – Horse Ford – Ryder's Hill – boundary stone at the head of the Western Wellabrook – down the Western Wellabrook to Huntingdon Cross – Eastern White Barrow – Western White Barrow – Red Lake Foot – Erme Pits Ford – Erme Head Ford – Plym Steps – Eylesbarrow – Nun's Cross – South Hessary Tor – North Hessary Tor – Great Mis Tor – Hanging Rock on the Walkham – Dead Lake Foot – Lynch Tor – Pile of Stones – Western Red Lake Foot – along the Tavy to Rattlebrook Foot – Rattlebrook Head – Steng-a-tor – Sandy Ford – High Willhays – West Mill Tor – Rowtor – Cullever Steps. It lay wholly within the parish of Lydford.

Over the years this boundary recognized by the Duchy has been in dispute in some respects with the boundary accepted by the commoners whose commons it touched. From the viewpoint of the Duchy there has been an encroachment generally to increase grazing at the Duchy's expense. The modern line of the boundary, coincident with that of the parish of Lydford, is as follows: Cullever Steps – Smallbrook Foot – Metheral Hill – White Moor Stone – Hound Tor – Wild Tor Well – Thirlstone – Hawthorn Clitter – Manga Rock – Stonetor Hill – Longstone – edge of Fernworthy Forest – Heath Stone – Water Hill Cairn – King's Oven car park – Walla Brook – East Dart – Dartmeet – along the West Dart to the O Brook – Dry Lake Foot – Ryder's Hill – boundary stone at the head of the Western Wellabrook – down the Western Wellabrook to Huntingdon Cross – Western White Barrow – Red Lake Foot – Erme Pits Ford – A Stone – Broad Rock – Plym Head – Plym Ford – Eylesbarrow –

Nun's Cross – South Hessary Tor – North Hessary Tor – Great Mis Tor – Dead Lake Foot – White Barrow – Lynch Tor – Western Red Lake Foot – along the Tavy to Rattlebrook Foot – Rattlebrook Head – Steng-a-tor – Sandy Ford – Curtery Clitters – Middle Ford – Cullever Steps.

The map on page 6 shows the two boundaries from which it will be seen that the differences are not great. It is probable that neither coincides exactly with the line of the original perambulation but that of the two the one accepted by the Duchy is the closer. The walk described in this book covers the boundary which the Duchy accepts as the historical one. Where significant differences occur between it and the modern boundary both are covered so that the walker may follow both routes or choose between them. It should be noted, however, that it will not always be desirable or possible to walk without deviation from point to point. Where deviation is necessary this is made clear in the text and in the sketch-maps.

PLANNING
THE PERAMBULATION

The perambulation is close to 50 miles in extent and can be walked in two daily stages by experienced walkers of a vigorous nature, and even in one day and night by the masochist who wishes to rush by without regard for history or scenery. This guide can certainly be used with advantage by those who wish to move along at speed. It is, however, primarily written for those who wish to perambulate in a far more relaxed fashion. There is no question on the moor, even in good weather, of thinking in terms of 4 miles an hour as a walking speed. An experienced and strong walker may do 3 miles an hour in fine weather for a while; an active and fit walker will probably manage 2½ miles an hour; the casual but reasonably fit walker should think in terms of 2 miles an hour. If in doubt as to whether one fits into even this last category then somewhere between 1½ and 2 miles an hour should be expected. The total time taken will also need to allow for stops for food, to commune with nature or to obey its calls and, quite often, to put on and take off waterproofs.

Equipment

The weather on Dartmoor can change rapidly and on the high moor the temperature falls sharply towards dusk. It is necessary to have stout footwear and to carry waterproofs and a spare sweater. It is a risk to suppose that a fine summer's day will remain fine. Given these simple precautions, however, plus a map and a compass, there is nothing in the perambulation to deter the normal walker. It should be noted of course that no waterproofs will keep out constant driving rain for many hours and no leather boots will keep the feet dry indefinitely. On the other hand, getting wet will do no harm so long as one keeps moving and warm.

The map recommended, and the one on which the names and spelling in this account are based, is the 1:25 000 scale (2½ inches to the mile), 'Outdoor Leisure: 28 Dartmoor' published by the Ordnance Survey. The heights on this map are given in metres.

Using a compass should deter no one and all the bearings given in the text are the actual compass bearings to use. All the user has to do is to turn the dial of the compass until the bearing stated is shown at the index pointer. Then, keeping the compass level to allow the magnetic needle to swing freely, turn round holding the compass until the red (north) end of the needle points to the letter 'N' on the dial. Then walk ahead in the direction of the travel arrow on the compass. In poor visibility it is advisable to check frequently that one has not strayed from the direction required. In good visibility it will be less tedious to choose a distant landmark in the direction of travel and to walk to it, then choose another and so on. Compasses, of course, are likely to differ slightly from one another in their calibration. Additionally, it is improbable that one can both set a bearing and walk to it with an accuracy within two degrees. Over a mile such a deviation will amount to some 60 yards. The reader should expect at least that order of deviation and, of course, more if the direction steered is treated more casually.

Ministry of Defence ranges

It *must* be noted that north of Princetown the Ministry of Defence has three firing ranges, Merrivale, Willsworthy and Okehampton. The boundaries of these are marked on the ground by red-and-white marker posts and by notice-boards. When firing is taking place red flags flying by day and red lights at night positioned at high points give warning of this and indicate that entry into these areas is forbidden. (It is not only forbidden but dangerous!) *Parts of the perambulation lie within these firing ranges.*

Advance notice of firing times is given in local newspapers and post offices and can also be obtained by telephoning Exeter 70164, Okehampton 2939, Plymouth 701924 or Torquay 24592.

Distances and access points

Six-figure grid references have been given to help locate places where cars can reasonably be left and other points of value to the walker. The first three figures are those which lie along the top and bottom of the map and the last three those which lie along the sides. Of each group of three, the first two figures correspond to the numbers of the grid lines on the map, while the third indicates the number of tenths to the right or above that particular line. The specific point located is at the intersection of the lines relating to these figures. For example, Cosdon Beacon has a grid reference of 637915. Car parking places are also shown on the map on page 6.

The distances on this perambulation are given in miles and yards for these are the units with which most people are familiar. The metric-minded will already know that 1 mile equals about 1.6 kilometres and they can convert into these units readily enough if they so wish.

In general a walker will wish to return to where the car has been left unless other transport arrangements can be made. Different walkers will have different views on the total distance to be walked in a day. They may also vary in their choice of starting point. It is not, therefore, feasible to suggest circular walks which would provide a different route to be followed on the return journey from that taken on the outward one. The map will enable the walker to plan his own trip back. It is worth noting that a return along the same line as the outward path will not prove at all dull. The viewpoints will be quite different and the 'ups' and 'downs', of which there are many on Dartmoor, will be reversed. In addition, the perambulator will be able to judge quite closely when it is desirable to turn back.

Stages of the walk

The walk has been divided into ten stages, for each of which the starting and finishing points are common to both the Duchy historical boundary and the modern boundary. Sketch-maps have been included for each stage to provide the reader with a convenient visual indication of the route and the main features described in the text. The 'Outdoor Leisure: 28 Dartmoor' map should be referred to for a more detailed view of the route.

To reach the starting point

The perambulation can be joined at any point on the periphery of the boundary but it is customary to start at Cullever Steps, Belstone. A good place to leave cars is above Belstone Cleave (G.R. 620934). The way to the Steps lies past the inn and up the hill to the Belstone treatment works of South West Water (SWW) which are on the right-hand side of the lane. The lane continues to Watchet Hill Gate leading on to the moor immediately past the house called Watchett (sic). It then continues as a well-defined track with Watchet Hill on the left with its military flag-pole. About ¼ mile past Watchet Gate the track divides with the main track keeping to the right towards the Steps. A grassy track, which is not taken, goes to the left towards Winter Tor. At this division in the tracks, the East Okement River can be seen in the valley on the right and the stone circle known as the Nine Maidens a little to the left. (The number nine does not refer to the actual number of stones in the circle but is an embodiment of the three-times-three mystic number. There are at present sixteen vertical stones and one stone lying on the ground.) Continuing on the main right-hand track, the walker will reach Cullever Steps after about a mile from Watchet Hill Gate. They are the stepping-stones on the beds of the East Okement and the Black-a-ven Brook. They are clearly visible, though sometimes under water, just upstream from the modern bridge erected by the army. The two streams meet a little downstream from the bridge. To the west of the bridge are two boundary stones marking the Okehampton and Belstone boundary. The larger stone has 'OP/B' on both the east and west faces and the smaller 'OP/B' on the east face only.

STAGE 1

Cullever Steps – Cosdon – White Moor Stone
(3.6 miles)

From Cullever Steps the way lies towards and along Irishman's Wall which can be seen on a bearing of 108° ascending the hillside between Belstone Tor to the left and Higher Tor to the right. It runs in the same line as the Harter enclosure wall seen just to the right of the Steps.

Irishman's Wall was built, it is believed, in the first few years of the nineteenth century, probably under the direction of a Mr Crawford, to enclose land unlawfully. Crossing records that 'Some years ago a project was formed by an Irishman to enclose a part of the moor here, and for the purpose of carrying out the work he brought a number of his countrymen to the locality. They set to work building the wall, creating no little surprise among the Dartmoor folk, and showing their contempt for the rough, damp ground over which they had to walk to their labour by going bare-footed. The men of Belstone and Okehampton said nothing, but let the work proceed. But they had, notwithstanding, no intention of allowing it to be completed. They saw that the taking in of such an immense tract would cut off their commons from the Forest. Consequently, when they considered that a fitting time had arrived, they met in force and made such breaches in the wall as to render it useless. The outworks of the Irishman having thus been carried by storm, he evacuated his position, and left the commoners victorious.' Mr Crawford has, in other contexts, been called 'the Scotchman' and it may well be that both terms are synonyms for 'foreigner', as often was the word 'Welshman'. The story is of interest since it seems that in the early part of the nineteenth century the wall was believed to follow the boundary of the Forest. If projected in the same line it would, in fact, run to the top of Cosdon.

The wall should be followed up the hill and down the other side. To avoid the worst of the clitter it is easier on the descent to keep the wall to the left and to follow the grassy track. At the bottom of the hill the wall crosses a track which, to the left, goes back to Belstone, and the wall also

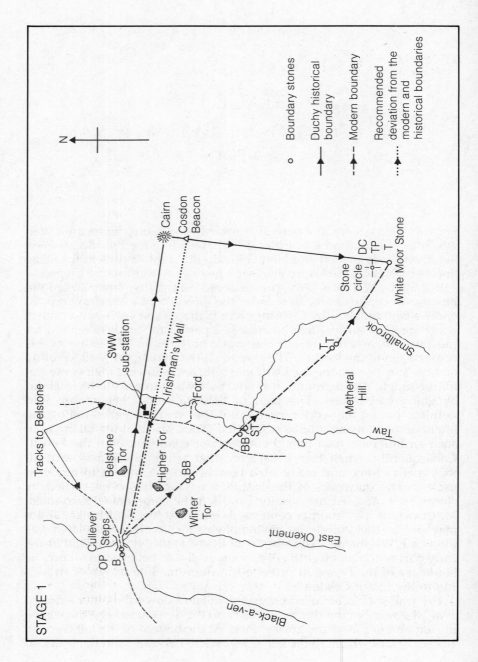

STAGE 1

Tracks to Belstone

N

- Boundary stones
- Duchy historical boundary
- Modern boundary
- Recommended deviation from the modern and historical boundaries

Cairn
Cosdon Beacon

SWW sub-station

Irishman's Wall

Belstone Tor
Higher Tor
BB

Winter Tor

OP
B
Cullever Steps

East Okement

Black-a-ven

Ford

BB
ST

Taw

Metheral Hill

T T

Smallbrook

Stone circle
DC
TP
T
White Moor Stone

passes an underground sub-station of SWW in which water from Taw marsh is aerated to remove much of the residual radioactivity associated with the underlying granite. The marsh itself lies just under a mile to the right. It will not be sensible to cross the River Taw at the spot reached by the remaining vestiges of the wall for the water will certainly be up to the knees. It will be necessary to turn right along the river, probably for 400 yards or so to an obvious ford.

Now comes a strenuous uphill section of some 600 feet of ascent over a distance of a mile to the triangulation point at the top of Cosdon. The Duchy line goes to the cairn 300 yards north of the triangulation point. Near to the latter are two recently built structures which are useful as wind-breaks but have no archaeological significance. The view from the summit is very extensive. Most of North Devon is revealed and to the SSE the Hameldown Ridge and the twin peaks of Haytor are easily seen on a clear day. The clearest days are those when an airstream from the north-west predominates and then the Bristol Channel, the English Channel by Teignmouth and the Exmoor hills to the north are all visible.

From the triangulation point the way lies on a bearing of 200° along a good and clearly seen track which descends gently to an inconspicuous tumulus on Little Hound Tor. There is much controversy over the name of this hill and the weight of evidence suggests that it should be marked as Whit or White Hill. The tumulus today consists of a few stones on a grassy mound possibly taken from the ruined cairn that may once have been here, although even that is open to question. The grid reference of the supposed tumulus is 631899. On the western side of the hill is a small rock ledge. However, the precise point of the tumulus does not matter greatly for the next landmarks are the prominent stone circle only 300 yards away and the associated standing stone which lies on a bearing of 157° from the circle and distant about 200 yards from it. The circle, which cannot be seen on the descent from Cosdon until over the hump of Little Hound Tor, is known as the White Moor Circle. In the last century the circle consisted of nineteen stones of which three were little more than stumps, the bulk of these three stones having been taken to serve as gateposts in the newtake walls of South Zeal common. Some stones which had fallen were set up in 1896 under the auspices of the Dartmoor Exploration Committee. Today there are seventeen erect stones, a fallen one and a depression in the ground which probably marks the site of the nineteenth.

The standing stone is known as the White Moor Stone and marks the boundaries of South Tawton and of Throwleigh with the Forest. It acknowledges this fact by bearing on its south face the letters 'DC' (for Duchy of Cornwall) and 'TP', and on its north and east faces the letter 'T'. It has been asserted on occasion that this stone was once part of the circle and was moved to mark the boundary but there is no evidence for

The two stones near Cullever Steps that mark the boundary between Oke-hampton and Belstone parishes

Belstone boundary stone near the River Taw; in the distance is Steeperton Tor

this and it seems far more likely that the stone is in its original place and is a menhir associated since the Bronze Age with the circle.

Stage 1 Alternative
Cullever Steps – Smallbrook Foot – Metheral Hill –
White Moor Stone
(2.7 miles)

There seems to be no sound historical basis for this alternative route to the White Moor Stone but it is the line commonly shown as marking the Forest boundary on modern maps. From Cullever Steps a bearing of 138° is followed to lead between Higher Tor to the left and Winter Tor lower down the hillside to the right. The ground rises steeply with much clitter and after ½ mile two boundary stones will be reached marking the Belstone bounds. The smaller bears 'BB/P' on its south face and the larger simply 'BB', also cut into the south face. A continuation on this bearing will lead the walker downhill to the Taw where, on its near bank, will be seen on a grassy knoll a stone put up in 1986 with the letters 'BB' cut into the east face. There are no prizes for guessing that these stand for Belstone bounds. The river can usually be crossed hereabouts with perhaps one boot in the water. On the far bank, at the confluence of the Small Brook with the Taw, will be seen another, much older, stone, with 'ST' for South Tawton cut into its south-west face. From this spot, the bearing required changes to 146° to lead across the flat Taw marsh; a small marshy hollow soon encountered can be easily skirted round. Taw marsh itself has been effectively drained by SWW.

The direction being followed leads up Metheral Hill to two South Tawton boundary stones each about 5 feet high and 20 yards apart, but these are not visible until nearly reached. Both bear the letter 'T' on their east faces. The direction now changes to 126° to lead over the Small Brook at a rather muddy ford and then up to the White Moor Circle and Stone.

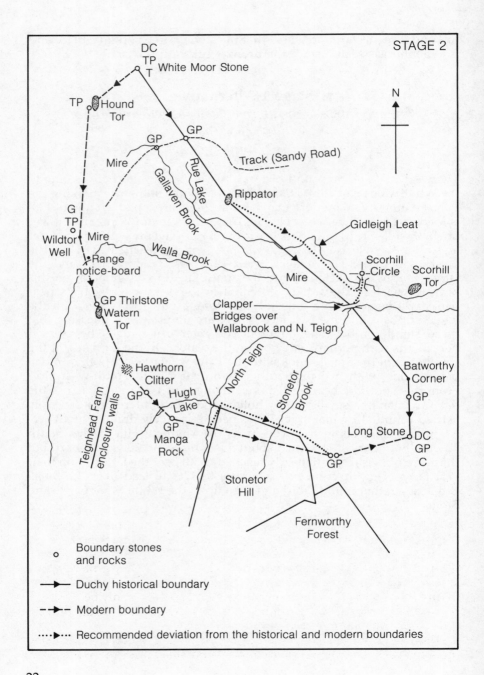

DC
TP
T White Moor Stone

N

TP Hound
Tor

GP GP
Mire

Track (Sandy Road)

Gallaven Brook

Rue Lake

Rippator

Gidleigh Leat

G
TP
Wildtor Mire
Well

Walla Brook

Mire

Scorhill
Circle

Scorhill
Tor

Range
notice-board

GP Thirlstone
Watern
Tor

Clapper
Bridges over
Wallabrook and N. Teign

Hawthorn
Clitter

Teignhead Farm enclosure walls

GP Hugh
Lake

North Teign

Stonetor Brook

Batworthy
Corner

GP

GP
Manga
Rock

Long Stone

DC
GP
C

GP

Stonetor
Hill

Fernworthy
Forest

○   Boundary stones
     and rocks

▶— Duchy historical boundary

--▶- Modern boundary

····▶··· Recommended deviation from the historical and modern boundaries

22

STAGE 2

White Moor Stone – Boundary rock near Ruelake Pit –
Teign-e-ver Clapper Bridge – Long Stone on
Shovel Down
(3.5 miles)

From the White Moor Stone a bearing of 146° for ½ mile over rather featureless ground covered with low heather will lead to a track known as Sandy Road though the name does not appear on the map. (The term 'sandy' is given to many tracks and fords throughout Dartmoor which often, but not always, have a sandy or gravelly aspect.) If the correct point of intersection with the track has been achieved a rock will be seen, slightly reclining, with the letters 'GP' for Gidleigh parish cut low down on the south face, though these are likely to be partly obscured by gorse. The rock lies on the near (northern) side of the track and is accepted by the Duchy as marking the Forest boundary. (Sandy Road, which is not followed, goes to the west to Gallaven Ford where a large flat rock also has the letters 'GP' cut into it. To the east Sandy Road passes over Buttern Hill.) The area to the south and east of the boundary rock is marked on the map as Ruelake Pit; the word 'pit' simply denotes a deep hollow. Ruelake Pit lies at the head of a small valley in which the remains of tinner's excavations are prominent. In the hollow rises the little Ruelake which flows into Gallaven Brook just under ½ mile to the south.

A small hill will be seen on a bearing of 154° from the boundary rock. This is Rippator or Rival Tor and is the next port of call. If the boundary rock has not been found it will not matter greatly provided that this bearing is taken from Sandy Road: the Road itself is a track not likely to be missed, though it should be emphasized that it *is* only a track. Rippator is about ½ mile away over rough and heathery ground with a few squelchy areas to break any monotony. The tor itself consists of a flattish slab of granite raised on a grassy knoll and can only be described as undistinguished. It will not be seen until the last few yards for it lies just below the summit on the southern side.

The view from this small hill can be surprisingly good on a fine day. Looking back the way we have come it is possible to see the White Moor

Stone against the sky. Steeperton Tor complete with its army huts and military flag-pole will be seen on 290°, Wild Tor on 262°, Watern Tor on 231° and the square pile of Kestor Rock on 134°.

The ground between Rippator and the Teign-e-ver clapper bridge is boggy and a direct line is inappropriate to put it no more strongly. It is more prudent to walk on a bearing of 123° until the Gidleigh Leat is reached in about ½ mile and then to cross the leat. This can be done in one easy stride and the leat should then be followed eastwards (downstream). Even so, boggy areas will be encountered but they are smaller and fewer in number than those on the other side of the leat. Here and there wooden planks have been placed to span some poor sections of the path but they are likely to be short-lived and, in any case, are not essential. The leat was cut some centuries ago, taking water from the Gallaven Brook, to serve Scorhill and other farms in the vicinity of North and South Creaber and Gidleigh.

Ahead, Scorhill Circle will be easily seen. It is, indeed, visible from Rippator, low down on the southern slopes of Scorhill. Gidleigh Leat passes within 60 yards of the circle and can be crossed easily at a clapper bridge of five slabs if the leat is followed far enough. While not strictly on the boundary of the Forest, the circle is well worth an inspection. It is a fine example of a stone circle of the Bronze Age not associated as far as is known with burial. The first known record of the number of stones in the circle was given by Samuel Rowe to the Plymouth Institution following investigations made in 1827-8. He reported that the stones were 'thirty-seven in number, ten of which are fallen'. Crossing, in his *Guide* of 1909, refers to a total of thirty-two stones, of which eight had fallen. The most authoritative account is by R.H. Worth who, in 1931, recorded twenty-three standing stones and seven fallen ones and conjectured that the circle originally had sixty-five to seventy stones. He also gave measurements of all the standing stones.

Today there are still twenty-three standing stones and seven fallen ones and a few vestigial remains which, presumably, were not included by Worth in his account. It is not surprising that the numbers recorded have declined over the years. The monument has been raided from time to time, in particular to maintain the south bank of Gidleigh Leat where stones taken from the circle can still be seen. Worth also records the catching red-handed of a man converting a fallen stone into a gatepost. Worth describes the incident succinctly: 'his desire was for gate-posts, but he had to obtain them elsewhere'. This stone is still there with clear marks of the frustrated attack upon it.

From the circle the way lies almost due south for 150 yards to cross the five-slab clapper over the leat already mentioned. The track then bears a little to the right and reaches the Walla Brook in some 200 yards and near to a single-slab clapper which is crossed. Along the Forest boundary, and elsewhere on the moor, various Walla Brooks and Wella Brooks will be met. All are derived from the word 'weala' by which the Saxons described their Celtic predecessors. It meant 'Welshmen' or more simply 'foreigners'. A few yards upstream from the single-slab clapper is the old crossing place of Walla Brook Ford, but the way now lies downstream for 100 yards to another clapper, this one consisting of two rough slabs with iron bonding, which spans the North Teign. This clapper replaced one swept away in the great flood on Dartmoor of 1826. There is some inferential evidence that the first clapper was put across the river not later than the early sixteenth century. The probable remains of this earlier clapper can be seen in the river bed and the adjacent bank 80 yards upstream. A further 80 yards upstream lies the ford across the Teign – the Teign Ford – from which the name Teign-e-ver is a corruption. The river at the ford is usually too deep to walk across and anyway the two clappers over the Walla Brook and the North Teign make the fords redundant for the pedestrian.

The confluence of the Walla Brook and the North Teign lies 40 yards downstream from the Teign clapper and in another 40 yards the walker will reach the point where the Batworthy stone enclosure wall descends to the joint river. Opposite the wall, and nearer to the far bank, can be seen a tolmen or holed stone. The main hole in the stone is about a yard in diameter. There is no particular significance to it for there are many such rocks with cavities worn in them by the action of wind, water and particles of gravel. In the past the stone was considered to be of ritual significance to the Druids, as were many of the natural features found on the moor. Today the ability to crawl through the hole without getting one's feet wet is taken, less seriously, to provide a cure for arthritis. Certainly the agility required suggests that one does not already suffer from the complaint.

From the river bank opposite the tolmen the way now lies parallel with the Batworthy enclosures and leads away from the river. (It was on the adjoining Batworthy estate that several thousand flint arrowheads, knives and scrapers were found in 1887.) At first the going is steep but the gradient soon becomes gentle. The enclosure wall is followed in its south-easterly direction to the end, a distance of about ¾ mile, when the wall turns through 270° to the north-east. This point is known as Batworthy Corner. To reach it the enclosure wall does not need to be followed at close quarters; the wall bends in and out and the ground very close to it is often badly broken up by cattle.

A little to the right from Batworthy Corner will be seen a stone row leading towards another stone row further up the side of Shovel Down. This first stone row can be followed and a little before its junction with the second row will be found two large fallen stones lying side by side, the further one having 'GP' cut into it for Gidleigh parish. Immediately

The tolmen, or holed stone, beside the North Teign; on the far bank can be seen Batworthy enclosure wall

after this boundary stone is a four-fold stone circle, none of the stones being of any great height. The only other such circle on Dartmoor is one, much restored, at Yellowmead near Burrator.

The next stone row can now be followed in the same southerly direction and this in turn leads to the vestigial remains of yet another row. At the end of this row will be found the Long Stone, the next point on the perambulation, but this will not be seen until one is close to it. It is, however, unmistakable for it stands some 10 feet high. It marks the meeting point of the parishes of Chagford and Gidleigh with the Forest and to denote this it has cut into its south face 'DC' for Duchy of Cornwall, in the east face 'C' and in the west face 'GP'. The north face is unmarked. There is little doubt that this stone is the one called Heighestone in the 1240 perambulation.

Stage 2 Alternative
White Moor Stone – Hound Tor – Wildtor Well – Thirlstone – Hawthorn Clitter – Manga Rock – Stone Tor – Long Stone
(4.6 miles)

This alternative stage marks the main difference between the route accepted by the Duchy and that recognized by the parishes adjoining the Forest. The latter take the Little Hunde Torre and the Wotesbroke lake of the 1240 perambulation to be the modern Hound Tor and Hugh Lake respectively. From the White Moor Stone the direction to Hound Tor is 230° over gently rising ground for a little under ½ mile. The tor cannot be seen from the stone though it can be seen from the circle nearby. It soon comes into view, however, as a pleasant grassy mound with protruding bedrock. The views from it are very good; Watern Tor, Wild Tor, Steeperton Tor, Hangingstone Hill and the Yes Tor range in the far distance, as well as many others, are all clearly visible on a fine day. About 70 yards past the tor is a boundary stone some three feet high with 'T/P' deeply cut into the narrow east face for Throwleigh parish.

From this boundary stone the direction is 192° over ground which rises very slightly at first before dropping to Wildtor Well. Just before the Well is reached the ground falls away and the rough grass gives way to extensive clitter on the lower slopes of Wild Tor. A bright green patch of mire marks the area where clear water oozes from the ground. This is the well, or spring, which we are seeking.

The mire itself extends towards the Walla Brook (the same Walla Brook already met at Teign-e-ver on the historical route) and is not to be trifled with. Hemery records the gruesome demise of a horned bullock there. Between the mire and the clitter lies a stretch of close-cropped grass dotted with rocks. It is a fine place for contemplation of the nature of the universe between sips of instant coffee and a sardine sandwich. The Walla Brook is seen coming down from the heights between Watern Tor on the left, prominently in view, and Hangingstone Hill to the right, the top of which cannot be seen. By the junction of the clitter and the grassy area, above Wildtor Well, there is a broken boundary stone measuring about 3 feet square and 12 inches thick, propped up at an angle by a stone. On its south face the letter 'G' is cut and the letters 'TP' upside down in relation to the 'G'. Presumably the stone marks a boundary of Gidleigh and Throwleigh parishes; I have not seen any references to it.

It is not sensible to make directly for Thirlstone for the ground is bad but there is an obvious track which keeps to the right of the poor ground and leads to a firing range notice-board which can be seen from the Well. The track crosses the Walla Brook a few yards upstream from the board and continues uphill to Thirlstone. Crossing states, 'This pile bore the name of Thurlestone in the thirteenth century, for there can hardly be a doubt that it is the bound named as such by the Perambulators of 1240. This name is supposed to be derived from the appearance presented by the two northern piles, which, when viewed from certain points, give the idea of being one in which is a large aperture, the *thurl*, or *thirl*, stone being thus the perforated stone, the term having its origin in the Anglo-Saxon *thyrelan*, to pierce. An arched rock on the shore of Bigbury Bay, between the mouth of the Avon and Hope Cove, which much resembles this tor seen from a distance, bears the name of Thurlestone rock, and this seems to me confirmatory of its derivation.' (However, just to confuse still more the boundary saga, it is worth noting that the White Moor Stone is also referred to in Ordnance Survey Boundary Report Books as Thurlestone.)

The letters 'GP' for Gidleigh parish are cut low down on the south face of the first pile reached of the two comprising Thirlstone. This spot commands good views, particularly back in the direction of Wildtor Well; the view of Kestor seen through the gap between the two piles is likely to appeal to most photographers. From Thirlstone the line of the boundary changes slightly to 163° passing the main piles of Watern Tor which lie further up the hillside and continuing to the enclosures of the old Teignhead Farm, reaching them a little south of the corner formed by the walls which run east–west and north–south. In Crossing's time there was a gate here but it no longer exists; however, the wall is easily crossed.

Within the enclosure lie several separate areas of clitter. Just before the last area of clitter is reached there is a boundary rock wth the letters 'GP' cut into the east face near the top. The letters are not deeply cut and

The Thirlstone on the modern boundary line; the two piles of rock appear as one holed rock from certain viewpoints the rock is not easy to find. I have seen no reference to it, though Hemery writes of a fallen bondstone in this general area of Hawthorn Clitter. The name of the clitter apparently derives from the trees which once grew there; there are none now. This boundary rock, however, is not a bondstone but a large piece of bedrock not dissimilar from, though smaller than, Manga Rock which can just be seen on the hillside opposite, bearing 142°, and to which we now make our way. This is the line to take from the clitter whether or not the boundary rock has been found. Two hundred feet of descent take us to the little Hugh Lake considered by many to be the Whodelake of the 1608 perambulation and the Wotesbrokelake of 1240. It is an undistinguished little stream hardly half a mile in length and seems a somewhat unlikely candidate to mark a boundary. Hugh Lake is easily crossed and about 75 feet of sharp ascent leads to Manga Rock, a large piece of bedrock with 'GP' cut into the north face. The rock cannot be seen from Hugh Lake. It commands good views of Kestor, Hound Tor, Cosdon and Fernworthy Forest. The word 'Manga' was probably a personal name.

From Manga Rock a direction of 106° will lead steeply downhill to the North Teign which is not deep there and should be crossed without too much difficulty. If there are problems it may be easier to go downstream for 300 yards opposite to where the enclosure walls meet the river (Mangersford Rails). Granite posts and some old barbed wire together with some dubious stepping stones mark the spot where the cautious may cross and remain dry. At whatever point the river has been crossed it will be desirable to go downstream to the Rails and to pass through a gate in the wall to the outside of the enclosure. (There is another gate in the other wall, with a barbed-wire fence behind it, which runs parallel to the river. This leads into the enclosure and can be passed through if the modern boundary is to be followed more exactly.)

One now turns sharp right to follow the enclosure wall which runs in a direction of 118° over Stonetor Hill. After ½ mile the little Stone Tor Brook is crossed and the way goes uphill to Stone Tor which is incorporated into the enclosure wall. Just before the tor is reached a slab of rock will be seen with drill marks on its edges.

From Stone Tor the direction to follow is 124° downhill for just over ¼ mile to two boundary stones which can be seen from the brow of the hill. The first one reached is unmarked but the second stone about a yard distant has 'GP' cut into the north face. The two stones are, rather unoriginally, known as the Two Stones. The reader may be glad to know that this second stone is positively the last Gidleigh parish boundary stone to be met with – that is if we do not count the Long Stone which has already been described on the Duchy route and to which a direction of 080° will now lead in ½ mile. The tip of Fernworthy Forest will be seen to the right.

The Two Stones on Shovel Down marking the boundary of the Forest and Gidleigh parish

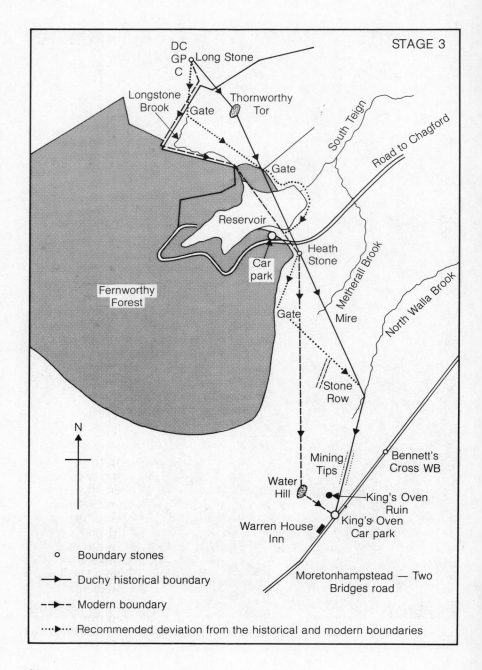

STAGE 3

DC
GP
C
Long Stone
Longstone Brook
Gate
Thornworthy Tor
South Teign
Road to Chagford
Gate
Reservoir
Car park
Heath Stone
Metherall Brook
North Walla Brook
Fernworthy Forest
Gate
Mire
Stone Row
N
Mining Tips
Bennett's Cross WB
Water Hill
King's Oven Ruin
Warren House Inn
King's Oven Car park
Moretonhampstead — Two Bridges road

○   Boundary stones

➤   Duchy historical boundary

-➤-   Modern boundary

......➤....   Recommended deviation from the historical and modern boundaries

STAGE 3

Long Stone – Heath Stone – King's Oven car park
(3.6 miles)

The presence of Fernworthy Reservoir and the uncertainty surrounding the original positions of the Heath Stone and King's Oven (Furnum Regis) make it inevitable that this stage can only approximate to the route likely to have been taken in 1240. From the Long Stone, the Duchy line would follow a bearing of 158° but it is better to go on 184° for that will not only avoid bad ground but will also lead to a gate in the Thornworthy enclosure. It will, in so doing, pass just to the left of a semi-recumbent stone shown on the map as the Three Boys; the other 'two boys' have long since vanished. Once through the gate the direction through the enclosure is 144° which soon leads across a small stream, the Longstone Brook, flowing south through old tin-streaming remains and into Fernworthy Reservoir. Doubtless in 1240 the perambulators could have proceeded on 158° which would have taken them without let or hindrance across Thornworthy Tor and eventually over Chagford Common. To do so now, following the construction of the reservoir, would result in an early end to the perambulation and to life altogether except in extreme conditions of drought. The direction of 144°, however, will lead safely across Thornworthy Down and towards the reservoir, which is soon seen, and to a gate near a copse at which the wire fence of the enclosure seen to the right meets a stone wall of the enclosure.

Having passed through this gate the walker will see the dam of the reservoir less than ½ mile away. The reservoir was completed in 1942 and covers about 76 acres. Obvious footpaths lead to a stile by the dam and further waymarked paths lead down through rhododendron shrubberies to a wooden footbridge which spans the South Teign below the dam. This is a most attractive spot, particularly in late May when the rhododendrons are in bloom. Usually, too, at this time of the year there has been sufficient rainfall for water to be flowing down the face of the dam.

Fernworthy Reservoir dam; in the background is part of Fernworthy Forest

The Heath Stone on Chagford Common

The footbridge is crossed and well-marked paths are followed up and back towards the reservoir, again through rhododendron shrubberies. These paths lead along the bank of the reservoir to a picnic area, a car park and toilets. The latter are closed in winter when the need is usually greatest but this should not prove of great moment to the hardy perambulator.

From this car park we turn left and leave Fernworthy Forest. From the cattle grid will be seen 130 yards straight ahead a prominent upright stone situated in the remains of a low stone wall. This is marked on the map as the Heath Stone and bears the inscription 'Jesus said I am the way the truth and the life S.E.P. 1970'. It was the reservoir superintendent, one Sidney E. Potter, who felt the need to pass on his religious convictions in this way. There is doubt whether this stone is on the line of the original perambulation. There is some evidence that the Langestone of the 1240 perambulation was further up the hill on Hurston Ridge and on a straight line between the Long Stone on Shovel Down and King's Oven.

From the Heath Stone the Duchy boundary lies on a bearing of 158° across Metherall Brook and Marsh to the North Walla Brook, but the ground on that line is very boggy and it is scarcely sensible to cross it except in unusually dry conditions. It is much better to follow the stone boundary wall of Fernworthy Forest in a southerly direction to the first gate – a single gate about ½ mile from the Heath Stone. From this gate the course to follow is 140° and this will miss all but a few patches of boggy ground. Birch Tor may be seen about 1½ miles ahead on the skyline. The North Walla Brook is nearly a mile distant and about half-way to it a stone row and standing stones will be seen to the right. The Bronze Age enthusiast may wish to deviate to inspect these more closely. Others may feel that one stone row looks much like another and plod on determinedly to the brook.

On reaching the North Walla Brook (which is really the upper part of the River Bovey) it is better to cross and to follow it upstream. The ground is much better that side and there is a path of sorts which follows the brook up through the old mine workings in which it rises. Eventually the Warren House Inn will be seen straight ahead and when it first becomes visible the mine workings at that point become broader and more grassy. From the top of the workings, and with the Warren House clearly visible, the site marked on the map as 'King's Oven (ruin)' lies 130 yards away on a bearing of 288°. It is an insignificant ruin on a grassy knoll. If the correct spot has been reached, two stones lying flat and side by side with a 'V' cut into each will be found 20 yards to the south-east. The original purpose of these stones is not known but they may have had a mining significance. King's Oven is the Furnum Regis of the 1240 perambulation but there is still doubt as to its actual position. The first

Ordnance Survey map of 1809 showed it to be where Water Hill summit is now marked. A law of 1198 required tinners to deliver their crudely smelted tin for a second smelting, weighing and stamping at a house 'at the hiring of the King'. Accounts suggest that in the early eighteenth century the ruin was far more impressive than it is today but was raided for the construction of mine buildings. Probably all that can be said is that the original King's Oven was in the general area of Water Hill and that the ruin now seen is more likely to be associated with a mine in operation in the early nineteenth century than a smelting house of the thirteenth century.

Whether or not the ruin is located, the way lies down to the main Moretonhampstead–Postbridge road, which is clearly seen, to King's Oven car park where there is a 'Guided Walk' noticeboard. This is a few hundred yards below the Warren House and it may well be that the perambulation temporarily loses its appeal in favour of fortification and the resting of feet at the inn. This was built in 1845 as the Moreton Inn and replaced an earlier inn known as New House which dated from the middle of the eighteenth century and stood on the other side of the road.

The modern line of the boundary differs a little from that of the Duchy. From the Long Stone it follows the Thornworthy enclosure wall to its junction with Fernworthy Forest and then runs close to the forest along to the reservoir. The ground close to the forest is particularly bad and this line, at least to the walker, has nothing whatever to recommend it. From the Heath Stone the boundary goes straight over Hurston Ridge to the cairn on Water Hill. In so doing it passes to the right of the stone row already referred to; it is always less than ½ mile distant from the Duchy line. From the cairn, which, as already noted, was in 1809 taken to be the site of King's Oven, the line runs downhill to King's Oven car park.

STAGE 4

King's Oven car park – Cator Common – Dartmeet
(6.6 miles)

From King's Oven car park the way forward is down the valley below the Forestry Commission plantation of Soussons, afforested after the Second World War and plainly seen ½ mile away. (The more distant plantation seen is Bellever.) Another Walla Brook, which rises just below the car park, has now to be followed and it is approached more easily by keeping to the western, right-hand side, of the valley and going at an angle down to the valley floor. The other side of the valley is a maze of the old Birch Tor and Vitifer mine workings. The brook is followed downstream and it is better to keep it on the left for the path is then generally easier. It can, however, be crossed easily from side to side, where patches of poor ground so dictate, for it is only a stride wide. It converges with the stone and wire fences of Soussons. After 1¼ miles the buildings and enclosure of Runnage Farm are reached and by then the brook must be crossed so that it is to the right. The brook is then left, but only temporarily, by a gate in the bank opposite to a small clapper bridge in Runnage Farm grounds. The farm is on the site of the ancient tenement first mentioned in 1304.

Getting through the gate may necessitate putting a foot into the brook when the water level is high; it depends much upon one's agility. A short way ahead will be seen a road which to the left goes to Widecombe and to the right to the Moretonhampstead–Postbridge road. A rather ugly modern bridge takes this road over the brook. It is best to cross this bridge and then to turn immediately left along the metalled road marked with a 'No Through Road' sign. This runs more or less parallel with the brook. Another ancient tenement, Pizwell Farm, first mentioned in 1260, will be reached at the end of the metalled road and here we need to turn left back towards the brook. This is crossed over some stepping-stones and the way continues parallel to a fence on the right for about 600 yards to a gate in this fence which is passed through. The way then lies on a bearing of 217° which will lead once again towards the brook. A

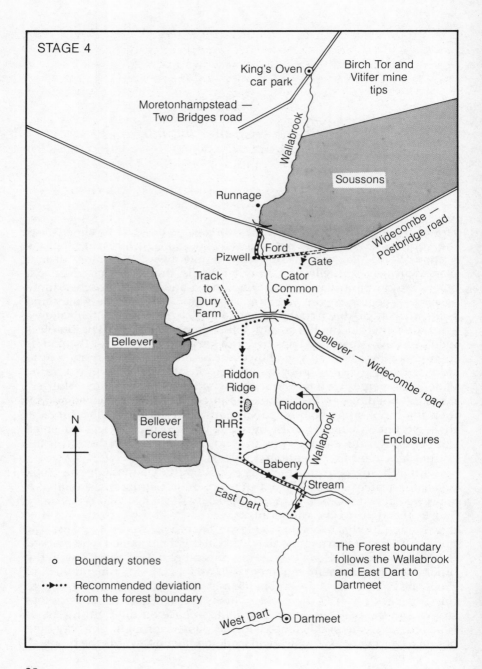

STAGE 4

King's Oven car park

Birch Tor and Vitifer mine tips

Moretonhampstead — Two Bridges road

Wallabrook

Soussons

Runnage

Widecombe — Postbridge road

Ford

Pizwell

Gate

Cator Common

Track to Dury Farm

Bellever

Bellever — Widecombe road

Riddon Ridge

Riddon

Wallabrook

Enclosures

N

Bellever Forest

RHR

Babeny

Stream

East Dart

o Boundary stones

••▶••• Recommended deviation from the forest boundary

The Forest boundary follows the Wallabrook and East Dart to Dartmeet

West Dart ⊙ Dartmeet

few boggy areas will be encountered and they are best skirted by keeping them to the right. All in all the Walla Brook and Cator Common, over which we are now walking, have little to recommend them and the former continues in its intransigence, as we shall discover.

The Walla Brook reaches the Bellever–Widecombe road where it flows under Pizwell Bridge; a gate a few yards from the bridge enables the walker to take his farewell from the common and to resume his uneasy relationship with the brook. To keep now to the right of the brook and close to it is almost impossible for the ground is abominable. To keep to the left is only marginally better and it will not be possible in any case to follow it along that bank all the way to its confluence with the East Dart for it passes through private enclosures. By far the best plan is to give it a wide berth and to go over Riddon Ridge. To do this, and to avoid boggy portions which extend for quite a distance from the brook, it is best to turn right over Pizwell Bridge and to walk along the road in the direction of Bellever for about 400 yards to a farm track signposted 'Dury Farm Campers Welcome'. From that point the direction to take is 186° straight over the top of Riddon Ridge.

The view from the top of the ridge is excellent. In the distance to the east can be seen the distinctive twin piles of Haytor. Much closer, to the west, and just across the East Dart, Bellever Tor and plantation are obvious. The prominent tor just to the left of the direction being taken is Yar Tor above Dartmeet. A boundary stone a little to the right of the line being taken may be seen marked 'R HR' on the south face, the 'H' and final 'R' being joined together. This is most likely to be a tinners' boundary mark.

About ½ mile past the summit of the ridge the ground will be seen to bear the marks of farming activity and the enclosure wall of Babeny Farm will be reached. A waymarked gate in the wall is the entrance to the farm. The correct line to take through the farm is both signposted and waymarked. Babeny is another ancient tenement and first mentioned in 1260. The farm is left by a gate across a metalled road and the latter passes over the Walla Brook which has meandered round in its boggy way to meet us once again. Any temptation to follow it immediately should be resisted.

The road should be taken for about 100 yards until it passes over a little stream. This stream should now be followed downstream and keeping it to the right: it will be seen to flow into the Walla Brook. Once again the brook is followed until it, too, ceases to enjoy a separate existence and merges with the East Dart. The way now lies along the banks of the East Dart beside boulders, tree roots and greensward to Badger's Holt and Dartmeet. Here is civilization indeed, especially on a fine weekend or Bank Holiday, so make the most of it for nothing else like it will be met on the rest of the perambulation!

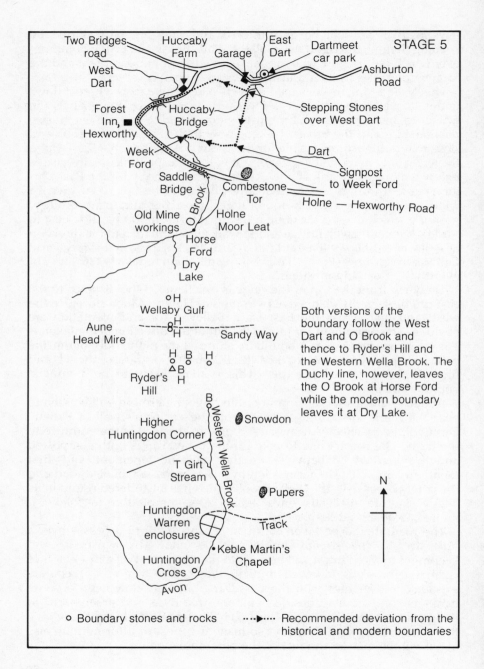

STAGE 5

Two Bridges road
Huccaby Farm
Garage
East Dart
Dartmeet car park
West Dart
Ashburton Road
Forest Inn, Hexworthy
Huccaby Bridge
Stepping Stones over West Dart
Week Ford
Saddle Bridge
Combestone Tor
Dart
Signpost to Week Ford
Old Mine workings
Holne Moor Leat
O Brook
Holne — Hexworthy Road
Horse Ford
Dry Lake
H
Wellaby Gulf
Aune Head Mire
H
8
H
Sandy Way
H B H
B
Ryder's Hill
H
B
Snowdon
Higher Huntingdon Corner
Western Wella Brook
T Girt Stream
Pupers
Huntingdon Warren enclosures
Track
Huntingdon Cross
Keble Martin's Chapel
Avon

N

Both versions of the boundary follow the West Dart and O Brook and thence to Ryder's Hill and the Western Wella Brook. The Duchy line, however, leaves the O Brook at Horse Ford while the modern boundary leaves it at Dry Lake.

o Boundary stones and rocks   ····▶···· Recommended deviation from the historical and modern boundaries

STAGE 5

Dartmeet – Saddle Bridge – Ryder's Hill – Western Wellabrook – Huntingdon Cross
(6.6 miles)

From Dartmeet car park the bridge over the East Dart is crossed and a few yards along the road is a garage. The path now required begins by the garage forecourt and is signposted, though the sign is only just visible from the road. The path leads through a gate into a field and much now will depend upon the state of the West Dart for this has to be crossed sooner or later. If we turn left from the gate down to the West Dart, stepping-stones will be seen. For most of the year it will not be prudent to use these. If it is possible to cross here, then the line of the boundary lies along the far bank of the West Dart, going upstream for just under a mile to the confluence with the O Brook. The banks of the West Dart are somewhat boulder-strewn and boggy. At the confluence with the O Brook there is a gate at which the signposted direction 'County Road, Saddle Bridge' should be followed between a wire fence on the left and the delightful O Brook to the right. It should be noted, however, that there is no public right of way along the West Dart to the O Brook, but there is from the confluence of the two rivers to Saddle Bridge which lies below Combestone Tor on the Holne to Hexworthy road.

For those law-abiding folk who have braved the stones across the West Dart there is another, though more circuitous, route to the West Dart–O Brook junction. On the far side of the river a track which is signposted and has waymarked stones lies straight ahead and this is followed as it rises between oak trees. The track passes through a gateway into fields and the hedge and wall is followed to another gateway near which will be seen a sheep-creep. This is simply a hole in the wall which enables sheep, but not cattle, to pass from one field to another. A bridlepath will soon be seen signposted 'Holne Road near Venford Reservoir' but this is not taken and the way continues to the next signpost. Here the direction marked 'Week Ford Stepping-stones for Huccaby ¾m' is taken. The way lies downhill to the confluence of the West Dart and the O Brook. (Week Ford has stepping-stones which also lead across the West Dart but are not relevant to this perambulation.) The way then lies uphill, almost back on one's tracks, to Saddle Bridge, as already described. Those who are more weary than perfectionist will readily see from the map that there is a quicker way to Saddle Bridge from the signpost marking the way to Week Ford, by continuing up to Combestone Tor, which is clearly seen from the signpost, and then turning right down the road. However, just under half a mile of the O Brook will then be missed and it is a most attractive half mile.

Generally it will not prove sensible and will often be dangerous to cross the West Dart near Dartmeet. At such times it will be necessary to take the signposted direction to Huccaby at the garage forecourt by Dartmeet. This leads diagonally across a field to stone gateposts, which are waymarked, and then sharp right between stone walls about 3 yards apart; boulders between these walls are also waymarked. The way continues over a waymarked stile, through a gate and then left at a signpost marked 'Huccaby'. A field is then crossed diagonally, in the middle of which is a post simply marked 'Path'. The way continues through a waymarked gate and 50 yards beyond the gate it is necessary to turn right to reach the road to Hexworthy opposite Huccaby Farm.

It will now be necessary to turn left and to follow this road, first over the unobliging West Dart, then past the Forest Inn at Hexworthy and along to Saddle Bridge. Unfortunately, this involves over a mile of road walking from Huccaby Farm. (Although Week Ford can be reached without going along the road there is no point in doing this because the stepping-stones at the ford which cross the West Dart will be more submerged than those at Dartmeet.) The tedium of the road, if such it proves to be, may be broken, time permitting, by 'having one for it' at the Forest Inn. The reader is urged not to risk the Dart when the river is running briskly; the inn has much more to offer than Dart water.

Saddle Bridge, which will now have been reached by one of the routes described, replaces an older structure taken down in the middle of the nineteenth century. The O Brook (a derivation of the word 'oak') is followed upstream from the bridge, keeping the brook to the right, for about ½ mile. A point will then be reached where the Holne Moor Leat takes its water from the brook; the course of the leat may be seen to the left. The leat was built some two hundred years ago to supply farms near Holne as well as a corn mill and a woollen mill between Holne and Buckfastleigh.

A little upstream from the leat/brook confluence is the site of Horse Ford which was once paved with flat stones on one of which was cut the letter 'H' for Holne. Horse Ford was washed away in a flood in 1965 and its site is now marked by a pile of boulders which divide the O Brook into two channels. The map should really show 'site of Horse Ford' rather then 'Horse Ford'. It is at this site that the dry channel of the old Wheal Emma Leat crosses the O Brook. The Wheal Emma Leat was cut in 1859 and taken more than 10 miles from the River Swincombe near Fox Tor Mire to the River Mardle to augment the supply of water to Wheal Emma copper mine, Buckfastleigh. The dry channel can be seen on the far side of the O Brook, contouring in its passage from the Swincombe.

About 400 yards past Horse Ford a stream comes in from the left – Dry Lake – and joins the O Brook opposite to some old mine workings; this was The Henroost tin mines, part of the Hexworthy tin mines complex. These workings can be seen just before Dry Lake is reached and if so desired, and the energy is in good supply, the O Brook can be easily crossed and the site of the water-wheel which stood opposite to Dry Lake until 1934 can be viewed. The pit housing the wheel was shored up by the National Park Authority in 1980.

The O Brook from Saddle Bridge up to Dry Lake, and indeed beyond, is most attractive and much favoured for picnics in the summer, particularly around the site of Horse Ford. However, farewells must now be made to the O Brook and the much less attractive Dry Lake followed upstream keeping the stream and the extensive mine workings to the left. The workings are almost certainly the accumulation of debris extending from medieval times up to the early years of the present century and are the 'Dryework' of the 1240 perambulation. The character of the moor is here very different from that of the O Brook valley. There is a path of sorts on the higher ground just to the right of the workings and this is followed going almost due south, always keeping close to the workings. Now comes a rather tricky bit. About ¾ mile from the O Brook and to the left of the path being followed is a boundary rock with the letter 'H', for Holne, cut into its east face. This is best found by observing the trees which live, though hardly flourish, in the mining remains. Once past the last tree, which will be sighted over to the left, the rock may be seen between the tree and the vague path we have been following. The rock is of no dramatic appearance to suggest that it is a boundary rock. It lies in a rather boggy and featureless area where the ground has opened out and the gradient has lessened. To make identification easier there is, fortunately, no other rock nearby. There is no harm in reiterating that the key to its location is that it is a little way past the last tree. If any other tree can be seen in the workings in the direction of travel then you have not gone far enough. The rock lies at the northern end of Wellaby Gulf, an old mining area mentioned as far back as 1542.

From this boundary rock the direction required is 185° over poor and featureless ground for about 550 yards until Sandy Way is reached. This is an obvious track running at right angles to the direction being taken

Stepping-stones across the West Dart

The junction of Dry Lake and the O Brook

44

and the area of intersection with it is generally accepted as being the 'Dryfeldford' of the 1240 perambulation. If all has gone to plan, Sandy Way should be reached at a spot where it is well marked with rocks. One of these on the near (northern) side of the track is a flat bedrock about 6 feet by 2 feet with the letter 'H' for Holne cut into the easterly end. This is marked on the map as 'B Rock'. Just across Sandy Way will be found a standing stone, leaning slightly, also with 'H' cut into its east face. This bondstone is known as 'Fieldfare' or 'Filfer Head' and is marked on the map as 'B Stone'. Great will be the satisfaction when these stones are found, especially if the mist descends.

It is quite possible, however, that they will not be located, either because the boundary rock at the northern end of Wellaby Gulf has been missed or because the nature of the intervening ground has not allowed very accurate navigation. All is not lost, however, if 185° is followed as closely as possible for that direction should lead to the top of Ryder's Hill (the Battyshull of the 1240 perambulation) or reasonably close to it. In the latter event the walker must seek the summit of the rather flat-topped hill. This is unambiguously marked by an Ordnance Survey triangulation point and two marked stones. One of these, Petre's Boundstone, is about 5 feet high and has the letter 'B' for Buckfastleigh cut into the north-east face. The other, which may be found lying flat or propped up, for it was not fixed when I last saw it, measures about 2 feet by 1 foot and has 'H' for Holne cut into it. It is known as 'Petre on the Mount'. If all has gone well with navigation then another upright stone about 3 feet high will have been encountered on the way up to the summit of Ryder's Hill. This is known as Little Anthony and has 'H' cut deeply into the east face. From here the triangulation point can first be seen.

The view from Ryder's Hill can be very fine. Nearest to hand are Snowdon Hill to the south-east, Eastern White Barrow (looking like a submarine conning-tower) to the south and the Red Lake spoil heap to the south-west. Further afield may be seen to the east the twin piles of Haytor and the sea at Teignmouth and to the north-west the North Hessary mast. It is said that the Isle of Portland and the Lizard Point can be seen on a really clear day but the walker will be very lucky if such a day is met; he should be thankful if the Red Lake tip can be seen.

The Forest boundary now runs on a bearing of 141° to another bondstone, just under ½ mile away, which can, with good eyesight, be seen from the summit of Ryder's Hill. This, known as the Wella Brook Stone, is some 5 feet high, shows drill marks down one edge and has the letter 'B' cut into the east face denoting Buckfastleigh Moor. It stands in a mucky spot marking the head of Wellabrook Gert in which rises the Western Wella Brook. The boundary follows the brook for its 1½ mile journey to the Avon. The brook can be followed on either bank but there is a balance of advantage in keeping it to the left. Old tin workings are everywhere to be seen in the gert. About 600 yards down from the Wella Brook stone the low earth and furze-covered stone wall at Higher Huntingdon Corner comes in from the right, running in a south-westerly direction. It marks the boundary of the old warren, of which more later. Just past the Corner more open-cast tin mining remains, known as T Gert, will be seen going back on the right in a north-westerly direction. The gert is home to the T Gert stream which flows to join the Western Wella Brook in a marshy area. Both the stream and the brook are only about 2 feet wide here and can be crossed easily from side to side to avoid the worst patches of ground. Across the Western Wella Brook and running back in a north-easterly direction is Gibby Beam, a working of the old Huntingdon mine. At about the place where the T Gert stream is first encountered, however, it is advisable to move up the hillside a little, for the ground close to the Western Wella Brook is not of the firmest, and so continue to the enclosures of the ruined Huntingdon Warren House.

The ground here, and in many parts of Dartmoor, is not conducive to natural burrowing by rabbits so breeding was encouraged by the preparation of man-made burrows or buries. These are marked on maps either as buries or pillow mounds and appear on the ground as mounds, often oval or rectangular. They were built with stone and earth and allowed natural drainage to take place. Many such mounds will be seen on the approach to the ruins. The original warrener's house certainly existed here before 1809 for during that year a lease was granted to Thomas Michelmore for the whole area of land forming Huntingdon Warren to be increased to 790 acres. A new warrener's house was then built and warrening continued until 1919. After that year the house was occupied intermittently and finally by a schoolmaster turned recluse. In 1956 it is said to have been accidentally made uninhabitable by a fire started by naval cadets and was demolished in 1961 on safety grounds. The house stood up the hill where will be seen a few trees. This is a delightful spot for a rest and a snack and to share the view with sheep and wheatears, which seem to have established squatters' rights, and with rabbits, which presumably have a longstanding tenancy. But anywhere in or around the enclosures is attractive and the ground is firm and close-cropped.

On the descent towards the Western Wella Brook a dry leat, which once took water from the Avon to the house, may be crossed, though this will depend upon how far up the enclosures one went to start with. This leat also helped to provide water, via the brook, to a water-wheel of the old Huntingdon mine which closed in 1868. Across the brook the ruin of the pit, housing the wheel, is prominently in view. The brook can usually be crossed without difficulty a couple of hundred yards or so

The ruins of Keble Martin's chapel near Huntingdon Warren

Huntingdon Cross, set up in 1557 on the bounds of the Forest and the manor of Brent

upstream from the wheel pit and it is worthwhile to do so because there, 20 yards up from the bank, can be found the remains of what is known as Keble Martin's chapel. It is not marked on the map.

The Reverend William Keble Martin, best known as the author of *A Concise British Flora in Colour* (1965), and his brother Arthur were among a group of young men who camped during the summer months in the years 1904–14 in the Wella Brook valley. They built this rough stone structure which measures about 6 yards by 4 yards with walls about 4 feet high. At the northern end of the ruin is an upright stone with a small cross cut into it. Keble Martin records that he baptized a child in the warrener's house and conducted evensong there. The warrener apparently supplied them with milk and eggs and the moor with adders but they suffered no mishap from the latter and doubtless their healthy exercise counteracted any cholesterol build-up from the former.

Having viewed the wheel pit and the chapel it is best to cross back over the brook and to follow it down for the short distance remaining before it flows into the Avon. Just above the confluence is Huntingdon Cross set up in 1557 by the Boundary Commissioners charged with surveying the bounds of Brent Moor then in the possession of Sir William Petre. Sir William was Secretary of State during the reigns of Henry VIII, Edward VI, Mary and Elizabeth; he was clearly a survivor, like his cross. The cross is unremarkable and has nothing marked upon it save some four hundred years of Dartmoor weather. Just before the cross is reached will be seen two old gateposts, one in the brook and one on its bank, which marked the entrance to the Huntingdon Warren enclosure.

STAGE 6

Huntingdon Cross – Eastern White Barrow – Western White Barrow – Erme Pits Ford
(4.4 miles)

The historical line of the boundary accepted by the Duchy goes straight across the Avon and steeply up to Eastern White Barrow, the Ester Whyteburghe of the 1240 perambulation. The barrow, as mentioned earlier, looks rather like the conning-tower of a submarine and can be seen prominently from the chapel and the wheel pit but not from the cross.

The Avon, however, cannot usually be crossed at all readily here. The walker will need to weigh the comparative merits of getting wet feet, and quite possibly wet knees, or walking an extra half mile upstream, crossing at the Huntingdon clapper bridge and coming back the half mile on the opposite bank. Of course it is not necessary to be such a purist: from the clapper a bearing of 146° will lead to the barrow. If the purist streak predominates then the bearing is 178° from opposite Huntingdon Cross and the way is much steeper. In either case, the barrow will not be seen until it is nearly reached.

Eastern White Barrow marks the southernmost point on the historical line of the Forest boundary. It is a fine ancient burial mound visible from many parts of the moor and itself providing a vantage point from which good views are obtained of the Red Lake spoil tip, the North Hessary mast, the Channel and, on a bearing of 290°, Western White Barrow which is the next point of call. It is worth noting here that the modern version of the Forest boundary goes straight from Huntingdon Cross to Western White Barrow, omitting Eastern White Barrow altogether. It has been stated, though incorrectly, that the Duchy accepts that version. There is no historical basis for the claim, but for those wishing to walk the alternative version then the bearing to take from the Huntingdon clapper bridge is 207° steeply uphill for ½ mile.

The ground between the two barrows is spongy and dotted with the old lode-seeking heaps of Bush Pits, now covered with whortleberries. The cairn on the top of Western White Barrow is home to the remains of

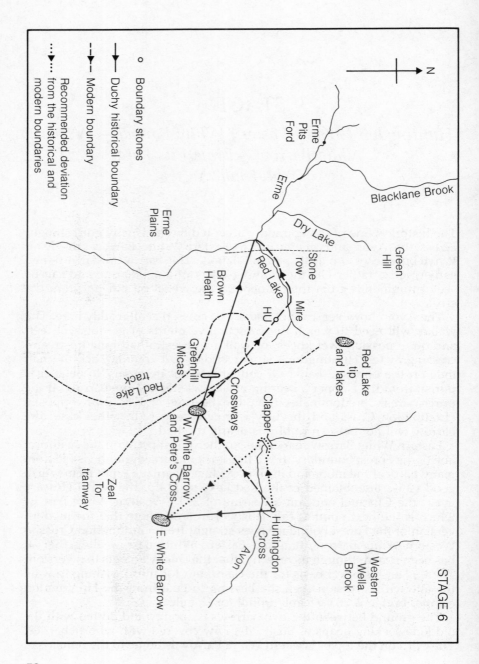

STAGE 6

Key:

- Boundary stones
- Duchy historical boundary
- Modern boundary
- Recommended deviation from the historical and modern boundaries

Erme Pits Ford

Blacklane Brook

Erme

Erme Plains

Dry Lake

Green Hill

Brown Heath

Red Lake

Stone row

Mire

HU

Red Lake tip and lakes

Greenhill Micas

Red Lake track

Crossways

Clapper

W. White Barrow and Petre's Cross

Zeal Tor tramway

Huntingdon Cross

Western Wella Brook

Avon

E. White Barrow

N

50

Western White Barrow; in the distance is Eastern White Barrow

Petre's Cross, another of the crosses set up in 1557. Both the cross and the cairn were much despoiled around the year 1847 by turf-cutters at the nearby Red Lake peat ties. This was not casual vandalism but occasioned by their need to build a shelter. The cross had its arms broken off to make it more suitable as a support for a chimney breast and much of the cairn was refashioned to form the crude shelter now seen.

The next leg of the perambulation, after about 100 yards on a bearing of 295°, passes over the slightly sunken track of the old Zeal Tor tramway. The tramway was built in 1847 to transport peat from around the Red Lake marshes to Shipley Bridge where naphtha was distilled from it to make candles for miners. The tramway was used at a later date to transport materials used in the extraction of china clay from Petre's Pits which lie south of Western White Barrow. The clay itself was conveyed to Shipley Bridge by pipeline.

If we continue on the same bearing the next features of interest to be reached are the filter beds associated with the china clay works at Red Lake. The beds in this vicinity are known as the Greenhill micas, probably named after an old mine once in that area. Green Hill itself is some distance away to the north-west. At the Greenhill micas the china clay slurry, pumped up from the works at Red Lake, passed slowly through baffles which removed the fine sand and mica. The clay remaining in suspension then passed into settling pits where water drained off. The clay, having reached the consistency of cream, was then released into glazed stoneware conduits, which can still be seen, and flowed solely by gravity to Cantrell near Ivybridge. The remains are extensive and many bricks lie around bearing the names 'Candy' and 'Hexter Humpherson'. The china clay works at Red Lake, from which all this activity sprang, started in 1910 and after many vicissitudes, including a change of ownership, closed in 1932.

The industrial archaeologist may be seduced by these remains, which are certainly of much interest, and temporarily abandon the walk in favour of a more leisured investigation. Those of a more inflexible nature will continue on 295° and will before long pass over the stony track of the old Red Lake tramway which conveyed men and materials by a steam locomotive of 3-foot gauge to and from the works. Immediately after crossing this track the walker will be able to see the Erme coiling its way down the distant hillside in the same line of sight. On a decent day the spoil heaps of Erme Pits are clearly visible along the river banks about a mile or so away.

The way now lies downhill over Brown Heath and the going is rather ankle-crunching. The line, if followed accurately, leads to the junction of Red Lake (the stream) and the Erme. However, the ground which would then be encountered is somewhat boggy and it will prove easier to turn a little to the right and to strike the Red Lake upstream. It can then be followed down to its confluence with the Erme. A short distance before Red Lake stream is reached a stone row will be crossed, quite clearly seen in the distance to the right where it extends up Green Hill; less clearly, a few stones will be seen to the left. This row, which stretches from Stall Moor to Green Hill, is just over 2 miles long and is believed to be the longest stone row in the world. The Red Lake is but a couple of feet wide hereabouts and can be crossed without difficulty.

Having viewed the confluence of Red Lake with the Erme there is no point in crossing the latter and it is better to come back away from it and to follow it upstream, keeping it well to the left. After Red Lake the next stream to be met is called Dry Lake. This is crossed and the Erme followed upstream until another stream is reached. This is Blacklane Brook, also called Wollake. It is most important that the brook is not followed upstream under the impression that it is the Erme. This is quite easy to do for the brook runs nearly parallel to the Erme just before the two merge and their junction will not be seen unless the Erme has been followed closely, and that would involve walking through very boggy ground. The Blacklane Brook should be crossed, which is easily done. There is merit, too, in crossing the Erme very soon after crossing Blacklane Brook and proceeding upstream with the Erme to the right.

Erme Pits Ford lies at the beginning of the extensive tinners' workings which will be reached some 400 yards past the Blacklane Brook. A fairly obvious track comes down to the Erme from the left at this point with less obvious tracks on the right (eastern) bank. It is not the easiest of places to identify with certainty but the fact that it lies at the very beginning of the mining remains should help.

The modern boundary differs slightly from the historical boundary. As already mentioned, it omits Eastern White Barrow. From Western White Barrow the line follows the old Zeal Tor tramway on 330° for about 600 yards to Crossways where the tramway intersects the Abbot's Way: this point is only some 100 yards from the stony track of the Red Lake tramway. The direction then changes to 311° which leads over that track and reaches Red Lake at, or near to, a boundary stone marked 'HU' on its south face, denoting the parishes of Harford and Ugborough. The boundary then follows the Red Lake down to its confluence with the Erme. From there to Erme Pits Ford it is coincident with the historical line.

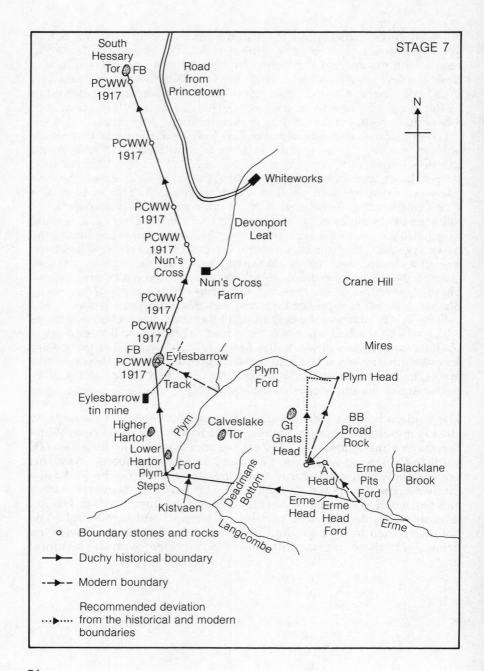

N

South Hessary Tor • FB
PCWW 1917

Road from Princetown

PCWW 1917

◆ Whiteworks

PCWW 1917

Devonport Leat

PCWW 1917
Nun's Cross

Crane Hill

■ Nun's Cross Farm

PCWW 1917

PCWW 1917

Mires

FB
PCWW 1917

Eylesbarrow

Plym Ford

Plym Head

Track

■ Eylesbarrow tin mine

Higher Hartor

Plym

Calveslake Tor

Gt Gnats Head

BB Broad Rock

Lower Hartor
Plym Steps

Ford

Deadmans Bottom

A Head

Erme Pits Ford

Blacklane Brook

Kistvaen

Langcombe

Erme Head

Erme Head Ford

Erme

○   Boundary stones and rocks

——▶   Duchy historical boundary

--▶--   Modern boundary

····▶····   Recommended deviation from the historical and modern boundaries

54

STAGE 7

Erme Pits Ford – Erme Head Ford – Plym Steps – Eylesbarrow – Nun's Cross – South Hessary Tor
(5.2 miles)

If the Erme has not been crossed already after passing Blacklane Brook as recommended, it must be crossed at Erme Pits Ford so that it is to the right. There will then be no risk of following the wrong branch of the river. Erme Head Ford lies about 400 yards upstream as the crow flies. Not being a feathered vertebrate, the walker will find the journey to the ford rather longer through the presence of massive spoil tips. It is important to keep these always on one's left and to keep close to the Erme. Erme Head Ford lies about 100 yards downstream from the source of the branch of the Erme now being followed. It is reasonably obvious from stones lying in the river bed and from tracks on the banks.

The Erme should now be left on a bearing of 284° and the walker will see from the map that this direction differs from the Abbot's Way which goes to Broad Rock and to Plym Ford. Whether or not our ecclesiastical predecessors ever used this route to pass from Buckfast Abbey in the east to Tavistock and Buckland Abbey in the west is not a matter to go into here. Suffice it to say that the earliest known appearance of the name 'Abbot's Way' was not until the 1790s when it came from the pen of one John Andrews of Modbury who called the track 'Jobber's Cawse, otherwise Abbot's Way'.

At first the way lies uphill then becomes more level and, in about ¾ mile, a small stream known as Deadman's Bottom is reached. This flows roughly from north-east to south-west and into the Langcombe Brook. Its grim name derives from the discovery there of a corpse two centuries ago. In 1927 another body was found in the vicinity, that of the young son of a workman employed at the Red Lake clay pits. The lad had been playing football with an older boy but they became separated in an autumnal mist and the younger boy perished before he could be found.

Deadman's Bottom is, in fact, crossed near the top and soon after this the Langcombe Brook will be seen to the left. The bearing of 284° is maintained and a good specimen of a kistvaen should be seen with the cover stone tilted back. Kistvaens are rude stone coffins, of which there are many examples on the moor. Worth measured a large number of kistvaens and found that most are about 3 feet long by 2 feet wide; this one is a typical example. Each side and end consists of a single slab of stone and there is a single slab as a covering. Many of the cover stones are missing or displaced for most of the kistvaens have been opened in the course of time. A little way beyond the kistvaen, the Langcombe Brook and the Plym meet at Plym steps. Whichever river is reached first should be followed downstream until it meets the other. Any errors made in leaving the Erme through failure to locate Erme Head Ford correctly will not then matter. At the confluence of the streams the Plym is on the right.

The Plym should be followed upstream for about 100 yards when a well-marked ford will be reached with obvious tracks on the other side. The river can usually be crossed here at no more than ankle depth. If it is too deep a crossing can be made further upstream and a return made to the ford. It should be noted that the ford in question is not that marked on the map as Plym Ford which is very much further upstream.

From the Plym the direction is 352° uphill to Eylesbarrow via Higher Hartor Tor. Lower Hartor Tor will be seen to the right shortly after crossing the Plym. Higher Hartor Tor affords good views of Sheepstor, Leather Tor, Sharpitor and Down Tor all to the west and north-west and, in good weather, the mast at North Hessary Tor just to the left of the direction being taken. Also a little to the left, but close at hand, are the ruins of the Eylesbarrow tin mine which was opened in 1815 and closed in 1852. The ruins provide a good spot for a rest and a bite to eat with plenty of rocks to sit on. Eylesbarrow itself is soon reached after leaving the mining remains and is distinguished by two cairns, a stone marked 'PCWW/1917' on its north-west face and a metal spike with an oval face, rather reminiscent of a cobra's head, embedded in a boulder next to the stone. The stone marks a boundary of the Plymouth Corporation Water Works catchment area for Burrator Reservoir. Though the latter was opened in 1898 the watershed was not purchased until 1916. 'Excalibur' has the barely decipherable letters 'FB' on one side. They are believed to stand for 'Forest Bounds'. If so, the effort involved in marking the boundary in this way seems rather ineffective; perhaps merely to have noted that it ran to the top of Eylesbarow would have sufficed.

From Eylesbarrow the direction to take is 026° on a broad and clear path marked at intervals with 'PCWW' stones. The path is boggy in places but these can be easily skirted. On the way down the gentle slope Nun's Cross Farm will be seen to the right with brief glimpses of Devonport Leat.

Nun's Cross Farm was built in 1870–1 by John Hooper and finally abandoned as a farm shortly after the Second World War. In those days it would not have been such an isolated abode as might be supposed for the tin mining at Whiteworks, only a mile or so to the north-east, was active if not flourishing. The farm, with its few trees, is a good landmark and a useful temporary refuge on a bad day. The nearby Devonport Leat, which is taken in from the headwaters of the West Dart below Wistman's Wood and from the Cowsic many miles away to the north, was constructed in the late eighteenth century to take water to Devonport. It now flows into Burrator Reservoir as part of the water supply for Plymouth.

A little to the left of the farm and on the path down from Eylesbarrow is Siward's or Nun's Cross. This old cross, referred to by the former name in the 1240 perambulation, stands about 7 feet 4 inches in height and has 'Syward' or 'Siward' inscribed on the east face across the arms. It is believed that the name may relate to Syward, Earl of Northumberland, who held property hereabouts in the reign of Edward the Confessor (1042–66). On the west face there are two words now generally accepted as 'Boc/Lond' and believed to mean 'bookland', that is land granted by charter and from which the name 'Buckland' is most probably derived. The cross must have been adopted as a boundary mark of the lands of Buckland Abbey for it preceded the founding of the abbey in 1278. On the west face there is also a small incised cross. Rowe records that in about 1846 the cross was overthrown and broken but was repaired and replaced through the initiative of Sir Ralph Lopes (who was associated financially with Eylesbarrow tin mine). The modern name of Nun's Cross seems to have been first recorded as 'Nannacross' in 1699. It is unlikely to have had anything to do with nuns and may have stemmed from a Celtic word for valley.

The next stage is quite straightforward and arguably the least interesting on the perambulation. The direction is 349° along an obvious track marked with 'PCWW' stones for 1½ miles to South Hessary Tor (the Ysfother of the 1240 perambulation): it seems much longer. The mast at North Hessary and glimpses of the Whiteworks to Princetown road are the highlights and the latter, which parallels the track, is visible only when nearing the Tor. There is another 'Excalibur' on the top of South Hessary Tor.

Syward's Cross mentioned in the 1240 Perambulation, now usually called Nun's Cross; in the background is Nun's Cross Farm

58

Stage 7 Alternative
Erme Pits Ford − A Stone − Broad Rock − Plym Head −
Eylesbarrow − Nun's Cross − South Hessary Tor
(6.0 miles)

The perambulators of 1240 named 'Grymsgrove' as a boundary point in this area of the moor and there has been much doubt over the years as to its location. It is now generally taken to be the position marked by the A Stone. This is a boulder, or perhaps more an exposed piece of bedrock, which measures, very approximately, 5 yd × 2 yd × 2 ft 6 in. It has the inscription 'A/Head' cut low down in its south face and is situated at G.R. 621673. The letter 'A' denotes 'Arme' which was the older name for the Erme. The rock lies in a boggy area which could be taken as the source of the river, though the area marked on the map as Erme Head is more definite (G.R. 622668). The exact source of a stream on Dartmoor is often difficult to define and many emerge from boggy hollows as a general seepage.

The modern boundary runs from the Erme at Erme Pits Ford on a bearing of 323° which will take the walker across the river. The A Stone is reached in about 700 yards. To find it the walker will need to check carefully the distance travelled, though it should be noted that few people have a stride as long as a yard, so it is likely to be more than 700 paces. The ground between is not too bad though it becomes boggy as the A Stone is approached. Unfortunately, the stone does not shout its presence and even the inscription may not be readily seen on a dull day. Any stone in the area should be examined by the intrepid explorer and not discarded hastily: the correct stone is an unlikely candidate among the other stones which lie within the general area.

From the A Stone the way to Broad Rock lies along 268° over gently rising ground for about 220 yards. This rock is also not easy to find. It somewhat resembles the A Stone but is smaller, measuring about 3 yd × 1½ yd × 2 ft high. It stands by the faint track of the Abbot's Way and bears the inscription 'BB/Broad Rock', the letters 'BB' being abbreviations for Blachford Bounds for it marks the manorial boundary. The letters are quite deeply cut and are unlikely to be overlooked even on a dull day.

The direct bearing required from Broad Rock to Plym Head is 018° but sources of rivers are seldom easy to locate with assurance. Any deviation to the right could result in the Plym being missed altogether and would lead to the featureless and unpleasant ground of Crane Hill. There is no future in such a proceeding. It is far better to go on 360° which will pass close to the cairn on top of Great Gnat's Head and then lead downhill to strike the Plym unambiguously downstream. It is possible that neither the A Stone nor Broad Rock will be found but if the distances and bearings given from Erme Pits Ford are followed carefully one should arrive safely at the Plym.

The Plym can then be followed upstream until honour dictates that the source has more or less been found in the rushes and peat. Signs of the past activities of tinners are numerous. The observant reader will have noticed that after Plym Head the way then lies back downstream to Plym Ford. Having reached the Plym on 360° he will have to make the agonizing decision of whether it is worth going upstream to an ill-defined position only to come back again. Doubtless the weather, the state of the legs and the degree to which the 'right stuff' is possessed, to coin an astronaut's phrase, will be inputs to the decision-making process. But do not risk missing the Plym by going too far to the right when coming over Great Gnat's Head or, without doubt, the weather will deteriorate, the legs will become weary and the 'right stuff' will seep away.

Once at the Plym there should be no difficulty in finding Plym Ford. Going downstream, and keeping the Plym to the right, an area will be reached with tracks which converge on the river and with extensive mine-workings on the far bank. The Plym should be crossed at the ford where it is only a few feet wide. A further 400 yards downstream a point will be reached where an unnamed stream comes in from the right which has its source amid the mine-workings lying uphill to the north-east. At the confluence of this stream and the Plym the direction to take changes to 303°, leading uphill to Eylesbarrow. A prominent track, which leads to the disused Eylesbarrow tin mine, will be crossed some 300 yards before the barrow is reached. From Eylesbarrow the way to Nun's Cross and to South Hessary Tor is the same as the historical boundary.

STAGE 8

South Hessary Tor – North Hessary Tor –
Great Mis Tor – Dead Lake Foot
(5.0 miles)

A continuation on the same track, just outside the enclosures, will lead to Princetown and to the Plume of Feathers Inn there. The strict line of the walk, however, now changes to 319° across the moor for just under a mile to the Princetown–Yelverton Road. Further 'PCWW' stones will be encountered. A smart turn right at the road will also lead to the Plume of Feathers but whether that will prove rewarding will depend upon the timing. The line of the perambulation, however, makes no such allowance for human frailty and goes straight across the road in the direction of North Hessary Tor. The way forward is to keep the small coniferous plantation to the right and to ascend the hill to the BBC radio mast; the latter is some 700 feet high. If the mast cannot be seen then it is tempting fate a little to continue. Discretion suggests waiting until a finer day dawns which, even near Princetown, happens from time to time. North Hessary Tor lies just to the right of the mast and is crowned with an Ordnance Survey triangulation point. The view from the tor is extensive and Crossing states that more than sixty tors can be seen. Those prominent in the forward direction include Great Mis Tor (334°), White Tor (326°), Roos Tor (310°) and Great Staple Tor (303°).

Great Mis Tor is the next port of call and the metalled road can be followed down to the Tavistock–Princetown road. The true line, however, runs just to the left of the metalled road and goes to Rundlestone Tor which is worth visiting. Just before the tor is reached a boundary stone will be seen marked with a broad arrow on the east face. The reader may well feel this to be apt in view of the proximity of the prison. He will, indeed, be right for it is related to the early acquisition of land by the prison authorities. On a prominent slab with a marked slope which forms part of Rundlestone Tor will be seen two rock basins which must presumably have been formed before the slab tilted.

The Tavistock–Princetown road is now reached either by regaining the metalled road or by proceeding through the enclosures which lie beyond Rundlestone Tor. The main road is reached opposite to a milestone which reads 'Tavistock/6 miles/ Moretonha/mpstead 14'. Eight yards in the Tavistock direction from the milestone will be found a boundary stone marked 'Walk/hamp/ton' and Lid/ford' on the west and

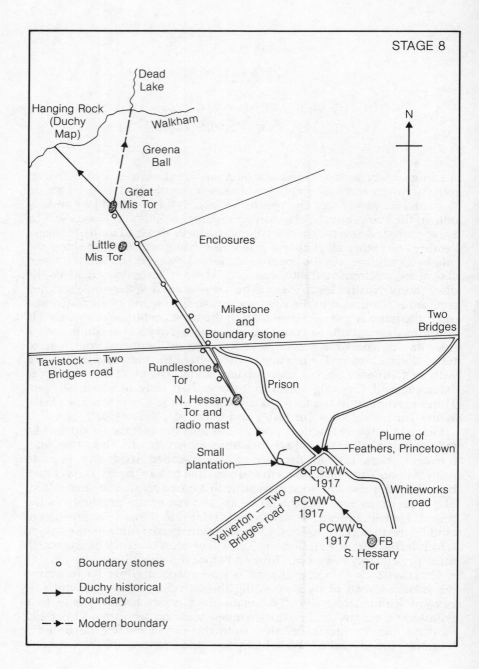

STAGE 8

Dead Lake

Hanging Rock (Duchy Map)

Walkham

Greena Ball

Great Mis Tor

Little Mis Tor

Enclosures

N

Milestone and Boundary stone

Two Bridges

Tavistock — Two Bridges road

Rundlestone Tor

Prison

N. Hessary Tor and radio mast

Small plantation

Plume of Feathers, Princetown

PCWW 1917

Whiteworks road

Yelverton — Two Bridges road

PCWW 1917

PCWW 1917

FB

S. Hessary Tor

o   Boundary stones

→   Duchy historical boundary

–►– Modern boundary

From Rundlestone Tor can be seen Great Mis Tor, the next point on the route

Limsboro' Cairn with its military flag-pole (see Stage 9)

east faces which are slightly inclined to one another. Opposite to this boundary stone, on the side of the main road first reached in descending from Rundlestone Tor, once stood a granite pillar known as the 'Great stone call'd Roundle' or the Rundle Stone. Crossing records that in 1881 he measured the stone and found it to be 7 feet high above the stones in which it was set and 4 feet in girth. It had the letter 'R' cut in relief near the top. Unfortunately, it was broken up not many years after when a wall was being built nearby.

Great Mis Tor is prominent about 1½ miles away. The track to it is signposted and leaves the main road some 200 yards to the west of the milestone mentioned above and opposite to an unmarked boundary stone. It starts just past the last two cottages on the main road. At first the track goes between enclosures and a number of unmarked boundary stones will be passed, some within and some outside enclosures. Little Mis Tor will be seen just to the left of the track. The Merrivale firing range is entered (on a non-firing day) and the summit of Great Mis Tor reached by the army flag-pole. At a distance of about 30 yards from the flag-pole, on a bearing of 352°, will be found the fine rock basin with a well-formed lip which is the true Mistor Pan. The first time it is known to have been mentioned was as long ago as 1291 in a Charter of Isabella, Countess of Albemarle. Like all the other rock basins on Dartmoor, the formation is due to natural weathering and not to the Druids or to the Devil: how unromantic are science and geology! Somewhat surprisingly, etymologists concede that the name of the tor may reflect that it is frequently enshrouded in mist.

The line accepted by the Duchy now goes on 321° to the Walkham, reaching that river at a point marked on the historical map at the Duchy offices as Hanging Rock. The line of the river is then followed upstream to Dead Lake Foot (G.R. 566782). There is, in fact, nothing on the ground which could be considered as Hanging Rock. That portion of the Walkham is singularly devoid of rocks. The modern boundary goes straight across Greena Ball from Great Mis Tor on 019° also to reach Dead Lake Foot but cutting out about a mile of the Walkham. The confusing part is that Hanging Rock is taken by other authorities to be opposite to Dead Lake Foot. Thus Crossing is quite explicit about the boundary and states 'We reach the Walkham at what is known as the Hanging Rock and immediately opposite to a combe down which flows a little stream called Dead Lake'. Hemery refers to a Hanging Stone at Dead Lake Foot on the south bank of the Walkham but also quotes from a statute of 1291 which placed it on the north bank. There is no prominent rock now opposite to Dead Lake Foot but there is a scar on the lower hillside of fairly recent origin which might possibly mark the site of the rock. Whatever the explanation, all sides agree that Dead Lake Foot is on the boundary.

STAGE 9

Dead Lake Foot – White Barrow – Lynch Tor – Western Red Lake Foot – Rattlebrook Foot – Bleak House
(5.9 miles)

It is now necessary to cross the Walkham and this can usually be achieved at Dead Lake Foot but after heavy rain it may be necessary to cross further upstream and then come back to the Dead Lake. The Dead Lake is followed upstream and after about 300 yards a well-defined track is reached (which runs from Peter Tavy to Princetown). A little further upstream the Dead Lake peters out amongst old workings and rushes. This is Dead Lake Head, or Dead Lake Well as it is sometimes called from the feeder spring in the shallow pan. Dead Lake Head is sometimes taken to be the Mewyburghe of the 1240 perambulation but the latter is more often, and more convincingly, regarded as White Barrow.

The Duchy line runs from Dead Lake Head direct to Lynch Tor but it is recommended that the walker returns to the Peter Tavy–Princetown track and then takes 022° to White Barrow. The track provides a more recognizable departure point than the rather indeterminate head of the Dead Lake and White Barrow will also provide an identifiable location – always an advantage in any walk on the moor. The course taken will never be more than 400 yards from the Duchy line. At first the ground rises slightly over Cocks Hill where long and tufty grass with potholes gives some variation. White Barrow will be reached in ½ mile but cannot be seen until nearly there. It is a low grassy mound with a few stones on top and lies on the Lych Way, a medieval track along which the dead were taken from the early settlements on the eastern side of the moor to Lydford church. In 1260, however, Bishop Walter Bronescombe granted permission to the tenements of Balbeny (Babeny) and Pushyll (Pizwell) for burial to be allowed at Widecombe church in view of the long journey to Lydford. This part of the Lych Way at White Barrow is coincident with the much more recent track from Peter Tavy to Walkham Head used for the conveyance of peat.

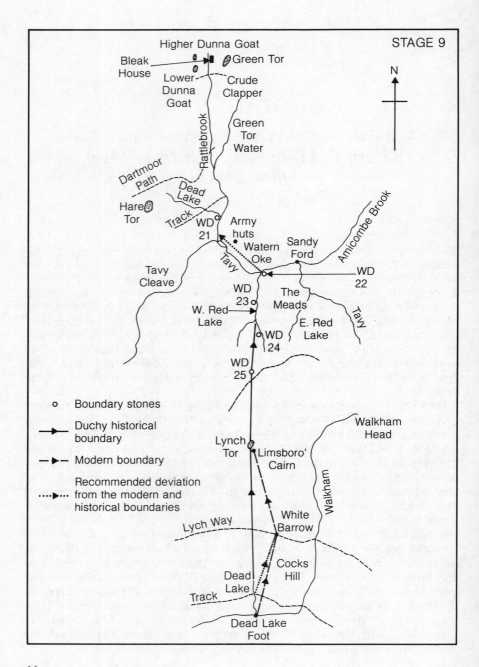

STAGE 9

Higher Dunna Goat

Bleak House

Green Tor

Lower Dunna Goat

Crude Clapper

Green Tor Water

Rattlebrook

N

Dartmoor Path

Dead Lake

Hare Tor

Track

WD 21

Army huts

Watern Oke

Sandy Ford

Amicombe Brook

Tavy

WD 22

Tavy Cleave

WD 23

The Meads

W. Red Lake

E. Red Lake

WD 24

Tavy

WD 25

Boundary stones

Duchy historical boundary

Modern boundary

Recommended deviation from the modern and historical boundaries

Walkham Head

Lynch Tor

Limsboro' Cairn

Walkham

Lych Way

White Barrow

Cocks Hill

Dead Lake

Track

Dead Lake Foot

As White Barrow is approached, Limsboro' Cairn and the military flag-pole upon it can be seen in the distance but they are only just visible from the barrow itself. Limsboro' is the southernmost pile of Lynch Tor and the bearing now required is 352°. Within a few yards of leaving the barrow the walker will find that Limsboro' cairn has disappeared but it will reappear in due course. In about ½ mile, at the half-way point, a tall, white and rusting steel post will be passed with, by the look of it, not many years of life to go. When in doubt as to its origin let us assign it to the military. Upon arrival, it will be seen that the cairn has been built around the tor and displays a good deal of pink granite. From the flag-pole, and in the forward direction, Fur Tor will be seen on 048°, Hare Tor on 346° and Great Links Tor on 352°, to name, as the saying goes, just a few. But do not stand too near the flag-pole or the compass bearings will suffer.

The next point on the perambulation was marked on the original 6 inch to the mile Ordnance Survey map as 'The Pile of Stones'. This was on not only the Forest boundary but also on the boundary of the hamlet of Willsworthy. The direction to it is 002° from Limsboro' Cairn but it is not marked on the modern map and neither will a pile of stones be seen upon arrival. What will be seen, however, is a granite stone bearing the inscription 'WD 25'. This marks a point on the boundary of land purchased in 1900 by the War Office from the Calmady-Hamlyn family, Lords of the Manor of Willsworthy. At the foot of the WD stone are a few stones which may be remnants of the original pile. 'WD 25' lies about ¾ mile from Limsboro' and just after a sunken track with stony tops to the banks is reached. The track was associated in the past with peat extraction from the area around Walkham Head. As soon as the track is reached it is recommended that the stone is sought and located, for it is useful to make a definite identification in this rather desolate portion of the moor.

From 'WD 25' a course of 008° should be followed and this slight turn to the right will lead to Homer, or Western Red Lake. Before the stream is reached 'WD 24' will be passed which is itself some 100 yards from a red-and-white military marker post which stands on the near side of Western Red Lake. There are numerous such marker posts in this area on both sides of the stream. There is no need to cross the latter which is followed downstream until it flows into the Tavy. On the way, and just under ½ mile from 'WD 24', there will come the thrill of meeting 'WD 23' and at the confluence, 'WD 22'. On a foggy day due obeisance should be made to these markers. The area in the vicinity of Western Red Lake is known as The Meads and the ground is neither good nor bad but just 'Dartmoorish'.

By 'WD 22' the Western Red Lake is crossed, which will be no problem, and then the Tavy by a series of boulders of various shapes

Where Western Red Lake joins the Tavy a stone marks the boundary of the Ministry of Defence land

The ruins of Bleak House, built about 1879 for the manager of the Rattlebrook peat works

and sizes which form a jumbled mass across the river. If the Tavy cannot be crossed here it will be necessary to go upstream for about ½ mile to Sandy Ford, where the Amicombe Brook joins, though even there it may not be easy.

From opposite to 'WD 22' the way lies downstream which here is in a north-westerly direction. Hare Tor with its military flag-pole is prominent and almost dead ahead. The purist will walk along the river bank through the extensive clitter, at much peril to ankles and legs, as far as Rattlebrook Foot. The prudent non-perfectionist will go over the hillside above all the clitter and will then have the benefit of seeing the remains of some of the ninety-four huts of Watern Oke which date from about 1500 B.C. These were first examined by the Exploration Committee of the Devonshire Association in 1905 under the guidance of the Reverend Irvine Anderson, Rector of Mary Tavy. Cooking stones, pottery, an arrowhead and a small glass bead were among the not very extensive finds. A little further on will be found two army huts dating from A.D. 1986. From the huts the course of the Rattle Brook coming from the north is plainly visible. The ruins of Bleak House and Green Tor are to the right of the stream and the two Dunnagoats, looking like a single tor, are to the left.

The Rattle Brook, though fast flowing, is quite narrow and can be crossed without much problem and certainly by the time Dead Lake Foot is reached where 'WD 21' stands resolutely on the west bank of the Rattle Brook. It is an advantage to do so and to follow the Rattle Brook upstream keeping it to the right for the track is much better there. Old tin workings can be seen along the banks of the Dead Lake and about 400 yards past 'WD 21' a ruined wheel pit of the old Rattlebrook mine is obvious on the far, east, bank. A little further upstream a track comes in from the left from the moorgate at Lane End, Willsworthy which probably was associated with the mine when it was operating in the middle of the nineteenth century. A few oak and ash trees are evident hereabouts. In just under ½ mile from this track a path comes in, also from the left, and fords the Rattle Brook near to where Green Tor Water meets the Rattle Brook on the far side. This path is the Dartmoor Path and leads from Brent Tor some 6 miles to the west. It was used chiefly by the workers at the old Rattlebrook mine.

The track beside the Rattle Brook continues through old mine workings and about 150 yards before the unmistakeable ruin of Bleak House is reached a prominent track comes in from the left and crosses the stream at a crude clapper. Bleak House, originally but less poetically called Dunnagoat Cottage, was built for the manager of the Rattlebrook peat works in, or about, 1879. This followed the building of a railway from Bridestowe to the peat diggings at Rattlebrook Head which lie ½ mile upstream. In the early years the trucks conveying the peat were horse-drawn but were later drawn by light locomotive. Bleak House is not a good place for a picnic, being generally rather smelly, fly prone and on the point of collapse as a notice on the south wall implies. It is, nevertheless, a good landmark.

STAGE 10

Bleak House – Rattlebrook Peat Works – Steng-a-tor – Sandy Ford – High Willhays – West Mill Tor – Rowtor – Cullever Steps
(5.9 miles)

From the Rattle Brook below Bleak House we continue upstream, keeping the brook to the right. Boggy and featureless ground is traversed, enlivened only by a boundary stone with 'L' on the south-east face and 'BS' on the north-west face. The letter 'S', if that is what it is, is turned on its side. These stand, one may safely assume, for Lydford and Bridestowe and Sourton and show that we are still on the Forest boundary. Walking will be easier, however, further to the left where there is a reasonable track distant some 150 yards from the stone which is marked on the map (G.R. 560868).

Rattlebrook peat works, or rather the remains of them, are now reached. The earliest extraction of peat there for fuel dates from the middle of the nineteenth century but it was in 1878 that the Duchy granted a licence to the West of England Compressed Peat Company for extraction. The history of the subsequent works is well documented by Harris who writes that it was 'a record of alternating enthusiasms and frustrations'. Extraction of peat for one purpose or another, which included the production of oil, went on until the middle of the present century. In 1961 the works, or what was then still left, were blown up by the army as they presented a danger to sheltering animals – which term one hopes was intended to cover walkers. Today 'Martin Leemor' white bricks lie around with other debris. The track which served the works can be seen running to the west.

The way still lies upstream for the head of the Rattle Brook has not yet been reached. It will be necessary, however, to keep well over to the left to miss very boggy ground; the division between poor and better ground is fairly obvious. In less than ¼ mile a track will be crossed coming down from Hunt Tor which has been visible from as far back as Bleak House. The tor is now quite close to the left. A little past the track a path of a sort leads across the Rattle Brook close to its head. The source itself can be located if the mood takes one. A direction of 063° is now

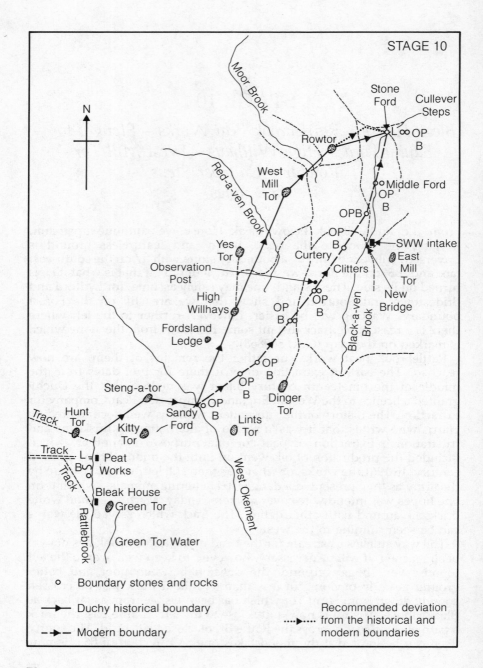

STAGE 10

Moor Brook

Stone Ford

Cullever Steps

Rowtor

L ∞ OP B

Red-a-ven Brook

West Mill Tor

Middle Ford
OP B

OPB

OP B

Yes Tor

SWW intake

Curtery

East Mill Tor

Observation Post

Clitters

New Bridge

High Willhays

OP B

OP B

Black-a-ven Brook

Fordsland Ledge

OP B

Steng-a-tor

OP B

Track

Hunt Tor

Dinger Tor

Kitty Tor

Sandy Ford

OP B

Lints Tor

Track

L B S

Peat Works

West Okement

Track

Rattlebrook

Bleak House
Green Tor

Green Tor Water

○ Boundary stones and rocks

━━▶ Duchy historical boundary

- -▶- Modern boundary

••••▶•• Recommended deviation from the historical and modern boundaries

N

needed to make for Steng-a-tor which cannot yet be seen. The tor which is visible a little to the right of this direction is Kitty Tor with its attendant flag-pole. Before long a military hut comes into view to the left of the flag-pole and then Steng-a-tor. The ground between Rattlebrook Head and Steng-a-tor is dry and firm until within about 50 yards of the tor when it becomes boggy; the whole tor is surrounded by poor ground. It does, however, provide a good point to view the West Okement valley with the Yes Tor–High Willhays ridge prominent and advertising the steep climb to come.

The most direct course down to Sandy Ford on the West Okement is 104° but the going is difficult with much massive clitter and an extensive boggy area close to the river. It is less tedious to take 110° for about 600 yards until a small stream is reached and then to follow this down to its junction with the Okement. The stream is marked on the map coming down from the direction of Kitty Tor. At the junction of the stream and the river, the Sandy Ford boundary stone will be seen across the Okement and only 5 yards from the bank. Here, or hereabouts, the Okement can be crossed though not without some difficulty. There are sandy spits in the vicinity though none is particularly useful for crossing the river. Places may be found where the river is sufficiently shallow with the water below boot-top level, but only just, In wet weather, and in the absence of 'wellies', this may prove to be a spot where it is better to take off boots and socks, roll up the trousers and endure numbed feet and ankles for a few yards. It will refresh the feet, anyway, for the steep ascent to come. The boundary stone at the ford is about 2 feet high and has 'OP/B' cut into the north face for Okehampton and Bridestowe.

It is now necessary to climb steeply through extensive clitter on 028°. Fordsland Ledge with a military hut will be seen to the left before High Willhays is gained. The latter is the highest point on Dartmoor at 2039 feet and the highest point in England until as far north as Kinder Scout in the Peak District. The climb of 700 feet from Sandy Ford is reason enough to admire the panoramic view. Yes Tor, with its flag-pole and Ordnance Survey triangulation point, is in the near distance along the ridge. It was long thought to be the highest point on the moor. Yes Tor is usually taken to be the 'Ernestorre' of the 1240 perambulation but the line taken by the Duchy does not quite pass through the tor but goes a little way below the summit, continuing on 028° towards West Mill Tor. This direction avoids the worst, but not all, of the clitter associated with the ridge tors. West Mill Tor is seen shortly after leaving High Willhays. A military track which runs from High Willhays to the army camp at Okehampton is soon crossed and then the Red-a-ven Brook which gives no problem. West Mill Tor is impressive and the views from it are singularly fine.

Rowtor, the next tor to be visited, is only ½ mile away and can be seen below the skyline on a bearing of 040° or thereabouts depending upon one's exact position on West Mill Tor. A track, the little Moor Brook and another track will be crossed on the journey to Rowtor. These join with the track first crossed below Yes Tor and it will be readily seen from the map that these tracks could have been taken to save going over the tops of West Mill Tor and Rowtor. If they had been there in 1240 it is probable that they would have been used by the twelve knights.

To avoid boggy ground it is now advantageous to make for the junction of a track and a metalled road where there is a red-and-white military marker post on approximately 050°, but again depending somewhat on the position on Rowtor. The metalled road in question is the second one to be reached; the marker post is easily seen from Rowtor. A right turn along the road will lead to a small timber bridge marked 'Light Cars only' which takes the road over the Black-a-ven Brook. This point is known as Stone Ford and another forest boundary stone marks the spot; it has 'L' for Lydford cut into the east face. Across the Brook, and near to the Harter enclosures, are two further boundary stones. One is larger than the other and both bear the inscription 'OP' on their west faces. These boundary markers are similar to, and of an age with, the stones first encountered at the outset of the perambulation from Cullever Steps. We are, indeed, nearly back at the start.

Stage 10 Alternative
from Sandy Ford to Stone Ford

The modern line of the boundary does not run over the peaks from Sandy Ford but takes a direction of 058° over ground which rises steeply and is dotted with patches of clitter. After ½ mile, which seems much longer, a boundary stone is reached. It appears to be a natural rather than a fashioned rock, measuring about 4 ft 6 in. × 1 ft 6 in. × 1 ft 6 in., and has 'OP/B' cut into the west face. It is visible from afar; on the way to it, Lints Tor is prominent close at hand to the right and Fordsland Ledge to the left.

A slight change of direction to 056° is now needed which will lead in about 400 yards to a piece of bedrock also bearing the letters 'OP/B' on the west face. It lies by the side of a grassy track leading, to the right, to Dinger Tor which is clearly in view with its army huts. High Willhays can now be seen to the left in addition to Fordsland Ledge.

The direction changes again to 047° and about ½ mile over flat but broken ground will lead to an obvious prepared boundary stone which stands some 6 feet high and about 18 inches square with drill marks visible. This too has 'OP/B' cut into the west face which, like all the stones already recorded and to come, stands for Okehampton parish

Sandy Ford on the West Okement; in the foreground is an Okehampton and Bridestowe boundary stone

Cullever Steps, the starting and finishing point of the Perambulation; in the distance can be seen Irishman's Wall stretching towards the tor on the skyline

boundary. By the side of the stone are the vestiges of another, much smaller, stone which retains only the letter 'B'. From these stones Yes Tor can be seen to the left.

Yet another slight reduction in bearing to 040° is now needed and the new line taken will slowly converge on a stony track coming from Dinger Tor and then cross it. About 300 yards after crossing the track two more boundary stones will be reached, one small and one large, both with 'OP/B' on their west faces. They lie amidst modest clitter and are easy to find as indeed are all the Okehampton boundary stones. Just beyond the stones a military observation post (number 3) is tucked into the hillside.

For some reason best known to the Boundary Commissioners, the direction required changes yet again, this time to 035° to lead in ½ mile to a boundary stone known as the Curtery Clitters stump. The ground between OP 3, which is passed, and the stump is not of the best and there is a small area of quaking bog just by the stone. However, there is nothing to worry about unless the walker happens to be a large lady wearing stiletto-heeled shoes, which seems improbable. The Curtery Clitters boundary stone is about 3 feet high and 1 foot square and has, believe it or not, 'OP/B' on its west face. On the way to the stone, East Mill Tor is prominent just to the right of the line of direction.

For once the direction to take does not change and 035° will lead again to the track from Dinger Tor which has curved round to run almost from east to west at this point. Although not on the line of the perambulation, if the track is followed round to the right it will lead very soon to New Bridge which spans the Black-a-ven Brook. This lies at the head of Rowtor combe and just above a SWW intake. It provides a pleasant area for a break in the walk and also a place where the odd car can be parked, for a metalled road from Okehampton passes here. New Bridge is a clapper of two openings which Page, probably rightly, thinks may have been built for the convenience of peat cutters: it is probably some two hundred years old. However, the true line of the modern boundary passes straight across the Dinger Tor track and reaches the metalled road just referred to at a boundary stone which measures approximately 3 ft × 1 ft × 1 ft. Here we meet individuality indeed for 'OP/B' is not cut into the west face: instead 'O' is in the north face, 'P' in the west and 'B' in the south.

Once again the bearing is reduced, this time to 026°, and in some 500 yards the Black-a-ven Brook is reached at a spot known as Middle Ford. There are stepping-stones here but in any case the Brook should not give too much difficulty to a crossing, which is now necessary to reach two more boundary stones, a large and a small, both back to the conventional marking of 'OP/B' on the west face.

These boundary stones stand in the line of the remains of a part of

Irishman's Wall first met at the outset of the perambulation. From here to the boundary stone at Stone Ford the direction reduces yet again to 020° over ground which is not bad though it has some boggy spots. To the Harter enclosure stones the direction would remain unchanged at 026°, crossing the metalled road a little south of Stone Ford.

Having viewed the Harter enclosure stones it is better to come back over the Black-a-ven and to follow it downstream, keeping it to the right. This last ½ mile downstream to Cullever Steps is one of the most attractive of the perambulation – and not merely because the journey's end is in sight. The brook flows swiftly, is overhung by rowan and other trees and sports several small waterfalls. It is a busy spot on Sunday in the summer; at least it is by the standards of Dartmoor. Where the brook flows into the East Okement we arrive back at Cullever Steps with Irishman's Wall extending up the hillside in front. What 50-mile walk could be as varied and interesting? It may well fire the desire to do it all over again, but going round in the opposite direction. If so, do not forget to add on, or to subtract, 180° from all the compass bearings given.

BIBLIOGRAPHY

Brewer, D. *A Field Guide to the Boundary Markers on and around Dartmoor* (Devon Books, 1986)

Crossing, W. *Guide to Dartmoor* (David & Charles, 1965)

Gill, Crispin *Dartmoor: A New Study* (David & Charles, 1983)

Gover, J.E.B., Mawer, A. and Stenton, F.M. *The Place-names of Devon* (English Place-Name Society, Vols VIII and IX, Cambridge University Press, 1969)

Greeves, T. *Tin Mines and Miners of Dartmoor* (Devon Books, 1986)

Harris, Helen *Industrial Archaeology of Dartmoor* (David & Charles, 1968)

Hemery, Eric *High Dartmoor* (Robert Hale, 1983)

Moore, S. and Birkett, P. *A Short History of the Rights of Common upon the Forest of Dartmoor and the Commons of Devon* (Dartmoor Preservation Association, 1890)

Page, J.Ll. W. *An Exploration of Dartmoor and its Antiquities* (Seeley & Co., 1892)

Robbins, John *Follow the Leat* (Published privately, 1982)

Rowe, Samuel *A Perambulation of the Antient and Royal Forest of Dartmoor and the Venville Precincts* (C.E. Moat, 1856)

Wade, E.A. *The Redlake Tramway and China Clay Works* (Twelveheads Press, 1982)

Worth, R. Hansford *Dartmoor* (David & Charles, 1981)

In addition, several volumes of the *Transactions of the Devonshire Association* have been referred to.

INDEX